Open to Fate

The Second Fountain of Fortitude

The 8th Fountain

(True Grace Version)

Robert J. Koyich

DEDICATION

To the muddled devotion of the notions to file.
Her smile crosses my countenance to the moment of denial.

CONTENTS

IT STARTS WITH A SEED

I know from my January 2018 trip that I want to live a better life than I've lived before. I appreciate the aspirations, ambitions, and earnings of a successful capitalist, yet have humanitarian compassion and like the idea of a guaranteed income for all. I also have some shackles and chains holding me back from success.

When I came back home from my January trip, my apartment wreaked of stale smoke. I've adjusted that behaviour by not smoking inside, yet I have been smoking cigarettes. When I went to bed the second night home, ideas about Seed parameters filtered into my mind.

I asked myself "how much rent can we earn from an 8-unit dwelling with PWD or welfare housing allowance? If the shelter portion is $375 a month, it means $3,000 can be collected per month which extrapolates to $36,000 per year.

After crunching numbers further, a Freedom Solution number is $15,128 per year; $1k/month rent, $50/week groceries, and $44/month bus pass. Even though my income at the time I started this book is near one Yearly Seed, my goal is to provide 1,000 of them for others.

For some first steps, I made contact with a Housing Development Coordinator. He and I met on Tuesday, January 30th, 2018, and I brought the numbers I wrote for Chilliwack

Seed and also my Introversial journals. I also contacted Ruth and Naomi's, a local street-level mission, for volunteering with them. Volunteering could hopefully let me get to know some of the people for whom Providing Point is meant to provide. Providing Point is the NGO idea I hold for Chilliwack.

Earnings are a vital part of this. At the point of January 2018 when I started writing this book, the total royalties earned from Amazon sales was $42.70. A long ways from the $4.5m/year needed to provide 300x Yearly Seeds in Chilliwack, and it reminds me that books will not be the only pathway to achieving Full Seed. Full Seed is complete coverage for all those in need.

Thinking towards the future, seed recipients shall also need to find channels and activities. The hope is people may be stable and secure without Providing Point support; similar to how I'm working for my self-sufficiency. Some people may want jobs, and some may attempt alternate pathways. If fully covered, future seed recipients may not have the ability or desire to earn their income past Providing Point support if we can achieve an entire Freedom Solution.

In January 2018, I signed up for a course with Ted McGrath. The premise of Ted's program is to use our story to draw in clients and apply lessons learned in life to provide programs for others. I'm not clear on what my experiences are yet, though I'm also, at this point, wondering about being a full-time coach. I prefer not to sell webinars or programs, and though it's an idea I've not yet tried, I also see public speaking as an avenue to develop and explore.

There's a need to clarify and hone my story and message. Ted's course helps with that, and it's in line with my training and learning, though I wonder who could or would use me as a coach. I also would like to have a coach to help guide me, yet at this point, the closest person I have for a coach is my cousin Alex.

Pivotal street people have known I've not yet provided much up to August 2018. In the future, Providing Point thrives, yet I strive to choose and fuse to pay my dues. The clues left along the shoreline rewind to *The Fountains of Yesterday* as a sign. Must I be money focused now? If my plow, our fields, and our efforts are to earn future yields, I must commit to the process to let our scenario unfold. I now know this journey includes vastly many more nodal points that just me, my wishes, and my books.

Diana had called and confirmed the Providing Point idea is a good one. She called it a '$5 idea.' The premise is that if each person gave $5 a month, we could house all the people who need and want a home in the Fraser Valley. 253 people are required to house and feed one person, a Yearly Seed, as a shared objective. Diana's guidance is helpful on this journey as she's patient, kind, and generous with her grace, information, and advice. I also love talking with her, and she's fun!

Open to Fate formed a lot slower than previous Fountains. I'm concerned about how this glacial pace of text develops, yet keep at it. I removed all my books from Amazon on February 12, 2018, and shifted Providing Points first earnings to be Patreon based instead of my books. The previous Fountains needed revision, though I still felt an urgency to provide; it's not a comfortable feeling.

It so often seems like I'm just at the start. We may be far from reaching the destination, though, in some ways, that's a positive thing. It makes me feel that although I've not achieved much, there is long-term potential. Perseverance is a thing, yet I also hope that it's perseverance and not a delusion.

A program I value, enjoy, and recommend is Toastmasters. Toastmasters aids me with evolving my communication and is part of the journey to Full Seed. There are multiple pathways in Toastmasters, and the one I chose is Team Collaboration. I prepared a speech for the February 2018 area contest that is a series of words that explains Providing Point and how it's to function.

I attempted to present my speech 'The Seed' and felt pretty awful about it. I tried to memorize the speech, though fell off course about 30 seconds into the presentation. I was agitated and solemn, yet I'm determined to make these projects prosper! I didn't recite the speech as intended though I refuse to quit and commit again to the process. To close this chapter, here is the speech I wrote in full, even if I didn't successfully present it at the contest.

The Seed

Do you think that each person deserves food?

Do you think that each person deserves a home?

Do you think that each person deserves necessary transportation?

If you think people do deserve that, how do you think we can help them have that?

Contest chair, fellow Toastmasters, and welcome guests:

I have an idea; it starts with a Seed

In a 2017 Report from by the Fraser Valley Regional District, 603 people were counted homeless in the Fraser Valley. Many people have complained about the homeless situation, though the homeless, I think, deserve our understanding, compassion, support, and respect. I write books, and in some of these books, I've written about an idea for a solution. The terms I use for this solution is the Seed Fund, and the goal is to achieve Full Seed.

Full Seed is entire financial support for all those who need food, shelter, and transportation. A Yearly Seed, the amount required for completely covering these individuals is $15,128 per year. A Yearly Seed provides housing, utilities, groceries, and a bus pass. Welfare and PWD (A disability income) are existing supports, though some taxpayers complain about "people that don't want to work."

Some people cannot receive welfare or PWD benefits because they don't have a home address and some others who need help have been denied. Even for those that are on Welfare or PWD, the $375 shelter portion is not enough to afford a decent place to live. We should not force people to help. We can't push someone to be compassionate or care; we can, though, help germinate ideas and share them as seed bearers.

It starts with a Seed.

I've talked about helping the homeless and those in need for a while now. Through 2017, Providing Point, the program I started to share from the Seed Fund, provided $250 of gift cards to people on the street to different businesses; Safeway, Tim Hortons and the Yellow Deli. Though $250 is far from providing full coverage for the first Yearly Seed, it is a start. In one conversation with a friend named Tim, he suggested the idea of what would happen if every person pledged $5 a month towards providing for the Seed Fund.

This idea takes root.

If there are near 296,000 people in the Fraser Valley, from the 2016 Census, and each person put $5/month towards the cause, we could gather enough money to provide 1173 people with a Yearly Seed; almost twice the amount needed for the current homeless situation. As of now, through an online site called Patreon, Providing Point has two people pledging $5 a month to go to the Seed Fund for those in need. $10 may not be much, yet it is a start. I note we need additional supports other than money, though:

It starts with a seed.

The first three financial goals for Providing Point through Patreon are small; $50 a month, $200 a month, and then $867 a month. For $50 a month, we can provide five $10/month gift cards locally, for $200 a month we may provide 20x monthly gift cards, though reaching the third goal of $867/month, we move towards sustainability. A Share and Care card is a pair of linked cards where a Seed recipient may hold one, and then Providing Point holds other. Providing Point shall put money onto the linked cards to provide for Seed card recipients. As we earn more, the $10 a month evolve to $10 per week and develop gradually forward to $50 per week for groceries. It is through these Share and Care cards that we can care for people's need for food.

What about shelter?

It's audacious to think that we can house every person who needs and wants a home, yet I do see it a worthy objective. If a Yearly Seed entirely covers a person's basic needs and is provided for by monthly contributions, 253 people can entirely shelter and care for a Seed recipient at $5 a month. Then again, some may pledge more.

I know numbers are a bit impersonal and may be overwhelming, though the math shows a possible solution. Some people pledge their time by volunteering, and that is helpful. Some can give their knowledge, skills, and expertise, and that is valuable too. For some, though, a monthly financial pledge is even more accessible and is a way to work towards helping those in need. The thing is, if we are compassionate people and want to help, we must step forward to do so.

It starts with a seed.

There are benefits to working together for a shared cause. We can make new connections and friends in addition to providing. We've learned and shall continue to learn much through Toastmasters as we learn how to convey our seeds to an audience. I know that most Toastmasters want to work towards a solution and though each of our clubs is a garden where we may live and thrive and grow, we should not forget what happens outside the walls of our club. We are called to be leaders and communicators and also to work for the betterment of our clubs AND our communities.

What would happen if the idea of the Seed Fund and Providing Point expanded outwards? What if other communities rallied together to support those in their areas towards and also achieved Full Seed? Are the ideas of Providing Point and the Seed Fund something that would take root in the gardens of other cities and towns? Are there enough caring and compassionate people that will work together towards a shared solution? Ideally, the answer will be to provide for all those in need, though how shall we do it?

It starts with a Seed.

If our clubs are our gardens, I ask you to also to tend to the fields for combined yields for our communities. The journey of the Seed is a shared journey, and this speech is a seed from my garden. It's to remind us each that we can, do, and shall help others in our life and world. It also is a reminder that we are fortunate to be part of an organization, Toastmasters, that builds and develops pathways towards a shared and prosperous future. We each are seed bearers, and Providing Point is my seed. We cannot make a seed grow, though we can help it to become.

It starts with a Seed.

Here is where it sprouts!

And though it seems the grains fell upon the rocky shoreline, perhaps the seeds shall germinate. Welcome to *Open to Fate*.

ROBERT KOYICH

A SEED TO A TREE

(February 27th, 2018 @ 6:44 PM)

This section, as most writing should be, is intentional. I wrote this section to share with people locally by printing it out to share in blue Duo-Tang binders. These few pages are meant to tell you what I'm doing and why, though it was much time before I completed the entire book.

The day before, the 4th Fountain rereleased on Amazon. I've written seven of these Fountain books, though had taken them all off Amazon because they needed additional revision. I used this book, the 8th Fountain, as a process point to clarify and hone my work and intents. It's used to condense my intentions up to now into a few pages to catch people up to where we are in the process.

I started writing the first book because of Natalie Imbruglia. When I was in the psych ward in 1999 and 2000-2001, the Natalie delusion and obsession was far stronger than it is now. In 2013, I started writing the first Fountain, *Finding Natalie*, with the intent to share the book with Earth and have her read a copy. The plan back then was for her to initiate a meeting with me, though this objective has drastically shifted since the first book.

The 2nd to 5th Fountains carried some ideas and notions about her, and though I still think of her, meeting her is not the mission I hold strongest. It was in the 3rd to 6th Fountains, I wrote a bit about the Seed Fund and Providing Point and presented promises and my Income Declaration. The responsibilities shifted since the original releases of those books, and as of February 27th, 2018, the commitments were being restated and solidified.

We live here in the Fraser Valley, and we know many people don't have a home in which to live. We also know that many people that *do* have homes and jobs that are just keeping afloat. For me, I know that I'd like to have a car and a house, though, with my current earnings, I can't imagine how. I also sense some strong displeasure from others because I don't have a regular job and have the life I have and live.

Still, though, I want to make sure we as a community can provide for others on the street and in need and also others who need or want extra support. I've made a lot of promises and declarations, and though not yet fulfilled, I work to honour these commitments.

As of June 2018, Patreon is the primary Providing Point income source. we use all money gathered through that page for Share and Care cards. I told you about Share and Care cards in the speech 'The Seed.' We started with individual $10 gift cards locally, though one of the next steps is regular monthly support. At the point of this chapter's reformation, we had $18/month pledged by four different sources.

At the point of $650 pledged a month, we can provide fifteen people with $10 *a week* Share and Care gift cards from the Patreon earnings. The first goal of $50 a month is for the first five recipients of $10 a month. It's a small goal in the long-term objectives of providing for *all* people, though we know it starts somewhere. It begins with a seed.

I know I have been overtly money focused sometimes. It's because I know money is a tool that we can use for others. A monthly $5 or $10 a month pledge is not massive. $5 is 1% of a person's income if they earn $500 a month; it's even less than a quarter a day. If you went to a church and tithed, you'd need to give the church 10% a month which is $50 for a $500 per month income.

Some people may contest they can't do anything to help the homeless. If 253 people pledged $5 a month to one person, that person could have $850 a month rent, $150 per month for utilities, $50 a week groceries, and a bus pass. 253 people to care for one individual whose life would be drastically different. If every person in the Fraser Valley pledged $5 a month, we could provide 1,173 people with weekly groceries, a home, and a bus pass. 603 were homeless in 2017.

I have preached a bit about kindness and compassion, and they're values I still hold. Some teach empathy, and that ability holds both understanding and compassion together. With insight, sometimes we can understand what it's like to be in a situation even if we've not experienced it. Most people don't know what it's like to be without a home, so how can some understand that? We still can have empathy. People without a home need the kindness and compassion *in action* and heart from what we do with those feelings.

Many people in Chilliwack know I've been muddled up with this bookwork and promise to earn for others. I know I've not provided the first home yet and I've been performing a lot of the work on my own. I haven't earned much support with the purchase of my books, and I've not been actively seeking donations and pledges. I don't like mooching, and wonder if it's necessary.

I obsessively keep working because I know this does hold value. I know I can't force a seed to grow, and it'll be awesome and fantastic to get some help for us to germinate these ideas and let them thrive!

Other than money or books, how can people help? If you don't want to contribute money, you can offer your skills or time. In Chilliwack, Ruth and Naomi's takes in volunteers on the last Thursday of each month, and you can call them to sign up. The Salvation Army is also a place to help with the soup kitchen and volunteering, and a third place, the Cyrus Centre is, a program that helps with at-risk youth.

I still bullishly believe that the best contribution I may

make is to tend the seeds, plant some fields, and remember to help out others when I can. We need to gather together and work in our communities no matter where we live; things do not often happen magically. If we are compassionate people, we must step forward and do something! Sharing kindness or a 'hi' and 'hello' are also great things we can provide, and donating items that we have at home that we may not need can be helpful too.

As one person, maybe the best thing I can do is be an advocate and share the seeds of giving and compassion. I've had a teetering balance between working for others, and also providing for myself, and though I've been working on books for about two years, I've not found much income from books yet either. I keep at it though.

Regarding tending the public fields, we also must not forget to tend our gardens. I remember Toastmasters as a place to gather seeds and share my ideas and heart with an audience I come to know. Both Wednesday nights and SnowPeaks are places to be and remind me our relationships are crucial and vital to ensure we can keep moving forward. By sharing the Providing Point idea and links, and helping with book sales, we can also help.

My plotting and planning include schemes to have Chilliwack a place where we can and shall provide for people with my work. Though I've been with the books for a couple of years now, it's only in 2018 that I shifted into advocacy and also founding Providing Point as a non-governmental organization to support. For those that are in lack or need, I want us to find people to help you.

Some friends think I'm a fool for wanting to help people, and some others think I should give my money to other charities. The thing is, I don't have money. When I can acquire some cash, I'd like to order copies of the books and share them locally. If it costs $80 to order a batch of 10-11x books, then selling them for $10 each is forward motion, yet only at a tiny scale. I'd prefer to find a more efficient means of support.

If we as a community can push Providing Point outwards to audiences outside of Chilliwack, could we gather for more than our local community? Would other companies and creatives put Providing Point ideas and practices in their communities?

It is a fundamental premise; if each person put $5 per month to those in need, we can provide good lives for others who need and want a home. Some people may contribute more than $5 a month, and that'd be fantastic! I can't 'fix' this situation on my own. It requires action by and from many pooling together.

Very few people have read my books up to this point, and I accept that. I'll keep gathering, sharing, and tending the seeds to ensure we may make a better situation for all. Even if I don't also have a clear elevator pitch to tell people why they should buy them, the books hold value. They are not classified easily as self-help, business, or are even entirely about social causes. Like the pages you have here, they stem from my dissatisfaction with how life is and has been.

They also are used as a conduit to share, collectively, how life can be. Every life *is* distinct and has its parameters, and the Fountains are written outwards to any who may want to subscribe to help other people or themselves. It's not a straightforward value proposition, though the ideas hold merit.

The Fountains books started as a form and wish for Natalie, though they've evolved past that and how I use them for therapy. The Fountain's earnings are used partly for social causes and also till the seeds of other people's lives and gardens. There is a hint for you; dream big and have a more substantial impact.

I'm happy, glad, and thankful that people read what I've written. It is an honour, a blessing, and an ultra-generous gift of time and attention. If I'm to gather attention for my books, though, I insist I must use them for a benefit beyond my wants. Some people have other motivations and use different tactics to achieve their desires, though I intend to use myself thoroughly well to earn and generate a shared Freedom

Solution; this is not only for myself!

If you want me to justify that position, I must argue that it'd be easy to earn a basic living just for myself. I could get a part-time job and ignore other people's needs, even my own. I see it as a massive challenge and more worthwhile to earn for many. If I set big hairy audacious goals of making enough to give away 99%, it gives me a much higher objective to expand, though, I also know I don't need that much.

I want to work and earn wealth, yet it's not fair for me to be wealthy if others cannot afford to eat. A lot of people would love to be rich. It's alluring and shared as an objective and element of freedom. If I have the opportunity and privilege to have my needs cared for, then I also must assure others too may reap similar benefits and rewards.

Setting massive objectives and far-reaching guideposts allow a long, arduous climb instead of just plateauing and accepting mediocrity. I work for others first. We must raise up those who need help while also working with those that want to assist us to reach our maximum potential.

Some may think it's me shooting myself in the foot before running a marathon to promise to help others, yet I want us to unify and work together. We need not put others down so we can reach the top, and we can lift up some when we level. I have a firm belief that by setting audacious an irrational goals we can become that much more together than if I just set small targets.

At this point, some people might say "It's not the destination, it's the journey." If I didn't set a faraway destination, then there wouldn't be much of a journey to get there. I know we're a long way away from housing the first person with Providing Point, yet I still deem it a worthy and challenging objective.

It's a lot different than when my primary wish was to meet Natalie. Reaching that goal would be so much less valuable for others. Sure, I'd get to meet her and talk, yet if I set my primary goal as Full Seed (providing for all people) and *also* get to meet her, it shall be an entirely different conversation than it would have been.

Natalie advocates for social causes too, hers is to end obstetric fistula, and I dare not forget that she also is working for many, and not just herself. If we work for others, we may hold a far more significant reward and effect than only earning only for our own basic needs.

Think now of the maple tree. The maple produces many seeds that slowly fall to the ground like a helicopter. The trees take a long time to grow, though when they do become mature, they need not be destroyed to tap them for their sap. The vital life of the tree is not lost to make use of them for something that is explicitly enjoyable.

It takes many years to cultivate the forest, though the trees produce something of value like the slowly forming streams of text. Can this be attuned to the syrup dripping slowly like the waters of life that may also nourish? Why do their seeds take so long to reach the ground!? Well, maybe waffles would be sweet.

I cannot easily describe the Fountains books, yet the tones of them are disjointed. The way this section formed is similar to how I've been writing in the past two to three years. I commit to writing a chapter, often in one sitting, and let the waters to flow out through the keys. Later I revise them, add some tidbits, and then revise again. The available Fountains have gone through multiple distillations before consumed.

I've yet to know how to describe my written work to others in a short sentence, though the ideas are strewn and spread out across the fields of text, and by reading, you are helping the fields. You pick up the pollen from the open flowers and giving a chance for seeds to form, germinate, and grow. The waters of life keep active to nourish the seeds; the Fountains are merely one source of water. With time, the seeds shall thrive, and then we tend them and cultivate the production. We may save some seeds to plant in other fields and gardens.

It starts with a seed, and these books are some seeds to share. There's not always only one solution to an issue, and often a resolution may not seem possible. If we are to plant the fields for combined yields, I give Providing Point and part of my book earnings as seeds to Chilliwack.

We must remember, though, that each community, not only our own, has people who need help. I'd like to create ideas and programs that can efficiently work in other cities, though where I started is Providing Point in Chilliwack. I'm learning, growing, and evolving myself, my work, and my ideas and intents. We know Chilliwack has fertile soil, yet I hope we may help you grow some fantastic things too!

LET'S BE HONEST

(March 8th, 2018 @ 9:43 PM)

Snowpeaks gathered tonight. SnowPeaks is the Thursday night Toastmasters group. I felt profoundly unstable, vulnerable, and exposed to fate. I also wish to infuse a positive future and write some of my life into reality. Some writers have said we can write our lives into being, though dare I cast some spells and fuse some of my invented ideas into text?

How may I construct my life from the point of seeming ultra-fragile into one of fortified stone? There is safety in truth and stating facts, yet "can you please tell me three truths?" Those three words asked as a question and request can be a valuable way to glean an introduction and a conversation.

When we request someone to tell us the truth about a sensitive or controversial matter, we may not receive honest answers. Insecurities can run deep and can additionally make the person feel uncomfortable. We might push some people away by pressuring them or trying to interrogate, and there also can be a lack of an answer to a tainted question.

Asking a person to tell you any three truths or facts openly is the idea; don't ask personal or pointed questions intending to find faults or fractures. Peace, love, acceptance, and openness can open up some exciting and positive dialogues.

The three profound truths that Lewis asks on his podcast *The School of Greatness* are different. Lewis' question is to ask for three vital life lessons or revelations to impact the world. My recommendation is to ask the person "Can you please tell me three things that are true?"

Questions are incredibly helpful to open up a dialogue. I've often noticed that when I talk about my life or tell people what I want them to know, I can quickly lose their interest or connection and a chance to communicate. It's an essential thing to ask questions, and they can generate beautiful things to discuss.

"How are you today?" is a radically good question to ask someone in my opinion. I believe that for a few reasons. Asking someone "how are you today?" allows a person to answer a question that isn't just a yes or no answer and can open up the context of his or her immediate feelings and thoughts. It's also not the question "how are you doing?"; a personal pet peeve of mine.

"How have you been today?" is also a good question and it gives insight into the person from how they respond. This question is about the person and how they've been up to that moment in time. The first question is more of an immediate check-in, while the second question gives the asker some guidance about how the other has been up to that moment in their day.

As I move forward, I don't know what my future holds. I am not consciously a prophet, and I positively cannot predict lottery numbers or tell a person what will happen even one day away from when asked. I don't often know the consequences of my actions are, though I remember that what I choose to do matters. There will be repercussions, results, and revelation from what we have done and shall do.

When I feel an extreme uncertainty or unease, I wish for the security to know what the future holds; if I will be safe and sound, if I will do the right things, or even if I shall see and hear from some people. When I encounter moments of deep insecurity and unease, I also train myself to build a definite sequence of events and allow myself to settle into peace. Like a feather or leaf, I like it to be peaceful in my home instead of causing a neurosis of turmoil from anguish or fear.

We develop and build our futures, and there are inevitable consequences from our choices. It's also true that we can attune new creations from and within these moments of uncertainty. I'm not clear how much personal information I should share in this book because I don't know who shall view it, yet hypothetical situations and theorizing are helpful to discern correct choices. Creative integrity guides me to want not to waste your time by reading.

My imagination about my potential audience also shows me subconsciously that I may be writing for your community too. I'd like to use my consciousness as a channel for many, yet my mentality somehow deceives me into believing none will read. My abundant thinking holds I don't need to write anymore, yet that is a lie too.

Motivation differs among individuals. If there are multiple influences and desires, one may be split between activities, contacts, and urges that seem to contradict. Using my thoughts as an example, the best way for me to write is to know more of my truths and consciousness than many others and then share it.

Rewind to the question "Can you please tell me three truths?" If we know what fact is for ourselves and we can tell another, and they understand and accept us, then bridging and bonding may ensue. *My* truths are hidden from my consciousness sometimes, and if I'm alone and unable to vocalize or write a coherent thought, I can't always bring my facts to the surface. If I dive deep into text and splurge forth a series of words that none other than myself see, then what is the point?

If we can discover new thoughts and ideas and then put them forward as a layer of text, a new truth potentially unearths. What facts would you like to share? What have you hidden in your being that looks back at you across the shallows of my mind? Does my sometimes warped thought find deep kindness in personal prerogatives and give you hope from my doubt?

Have we made the right choice? Will my voice hold an immeasurably higher value than my fragmented, trite, and self-depreciating words? Is the use of writing out my thoughts vastly better than telling you to your face exactly what I mean? Are my truths crystals of mana that covertly radiate into the fabric of time; adding even one extra space or two periods after the rhyme? Full stop. I still don't know.

If I'm honest, then I must heed the advice about adjusting goals, behaviours, and my truths. If I have faith, hope, and belief, then I also must be honest. Compounding upon the premise of honesty, should I also tell you my expectations?

Someone else said to me they think I have an abundant mindset, yet please also be rational and look at my results and fantasies. $15,128 per person per year to support and cover a person's living wage. My stated goal: To provide 1,000 people Yearly Seeds from my earnings. My results up to release are $68.26 royalties from Amazon in about two years of authorship. A drastic difference.

If I am to adjust my goals to meet reality, then is it best to adapt and change my objectives? Bullishly I want to refuse a change, yet experimental comprehension and curiosity guide this section to a different state of goals. The goals may be, and yes I put this in mocking quotes, 'rational.'

Before I tell you what my rational goals are, I also must include a premise and word. PLU8R is an extension of a raver credo of PLUR; peace, love, unity, and respect. I added an eight due to multiple other R-words in my version. There are more than a dozen R-Words used in the credo, and I include them in the 9th Fountain as chapter headings.

Rationalization is a word of the extended credo and philosophy, yet I feel confident to say that rationalization doesn't mean we should be making excuses or be rational. Rationalization is a PLU8R idea by making sense of one's set of beliefs or thoughts. Recognition is a PLU8R word, yet I use the word in the philosophy on the premise of recognizing in the definition of identification. If I hear a voice in my mind, and I can understand who it is, then I can adjust my consciousness into Respect for the person.

I can also, if to channel a person's voice, work with Representation to either convey what they would say, to represent them, or to understand what that person would communicate with their view. The signs of Representation can be fromed from the moment before. It's a bit convoluted, though I attempt to restructure.

I've felt negative energy towards myself and from myself for being rational. I've been heeding too much of what I've been told to do instead of being truthful, honest, and in alignment with who I am. My irrational side may allow magnificent and impressive things to manifest and materialize, though I have fears of limiting myself.

If I don't set audacious goals I may accomplish nothing and submit to a life I'd regret, so I almost defiantly wish to assert irrational thinking. I reach goals because my instinct tells me having them will assure a more favourable result than, as they say, thinking small.

If I'm to hone my goals, energy, and objectives in a more rational way, then could I also easily achieve what I want if I clarify precisely what that is? A metaphor or analogy for this? I immediately think of the lottery. If I have $5, I could bank it all on a lottery ticket and win 50 million dollars. I have $5, and if I bet my entire creative earnings into the chance that they will house 1,000 people, I could instead end up with exactly what I can predict for myself now, a cup of coffee.

If I use predictive abilities and fuse my wants into a more logical plan of possible action, though, then perchance I can reduce frustration, anxiety, and dismay by lowering my desires. I have my home, and I also, since starting this book, live with Zeus, the cat. I have a computer that I can write on, and I have cigarettes at this point too. I can't quite imagine how life being a non-smoker is as tobacco has been part of my everyday reality for 25 years.

My paranoid side also is the truth. Even if I believe in

God, my belief holds that I can easily be used or manipulated for His agenda. My life is not something I can assure is safe, guarded, and protected, and I know God has used people as martyrs before. My lack of obedience, understanding, repentance, and penance are not something I've trusted in well enough. I lack awareness, yet wish for faith and courage.

Magic is a thing, yet I don't mean the mystical spiritual form or the fantastic illusionary display. I mean Magic very plainly as a reference to the trading card game. The people that play or have played Magic are not evil; it's a good game. Magic also is a base from which I've derived from much of my codes and understanding.

The systems and actualization of my reality fuse with and from Magic's ideas and guide the book *Nodal Input*. In the game, there are five primary colours whose symbology is rational for non-magic players and those who don't even know the game exists.

The blue mana symbol is a water drop. Water is universal in human awareness. The red mana symbol is fire, and we know most know anger can be a red word. People could also understand that forests are the colour green, yet green can be marijuana or money. In Magic, black mana is associated with death and decay (cigarettes), while the white mana symbol, a sun, signifies order and protection. The symbology cues up my cognitive awareness.

The intricacies of my codes with Magic don't quite make sense to Magic players, though. My understanding of colour, language, and math unify in my comprehension, yet even when rationally explained to another can confuse or seem like nonsense. As I learn *how* to share my subvert ideas with others in ways that make sense, the network of cognitive thought shifts and changes.

I don't want to override other people's beliefs, yet it's also cryptically clear that when I gather shards of thought and present them logically, that new pathways emerge. I've been told not to apologize or vocalize my mistakes, yet I ask; isn't repentance a way towards atoning and straightening out ideas of truth?

If I make an assumption, and act upon it as fact, should I not let the other person know what the truth is and not acknowledge the falsity? If I can gather and share vital information instead, and present it in a way that people understand, could that aid in comprehension and avoid misinterpretation? If I told someone exactly what I meant and mean, how would that change the course of events for them?

I was meant to be telling you, though, about a logical path of what I want that is within reach. I fell away from that. Futures collaborate with the gates above and below without towing anyone into the moment of how. I am a plow, the words are the seeds, and though if I am a seed, what shall I produce?

Some of the terms I use from other people's books, works, and podcasts are like stolen grain. Maybe you don't want me to process the wheat to make bread, and I cannot assure I'll be alive in forty years from now. It's a wish, yet I can't even guarantee life or that I support myself let alone others.

I'd like to tell you what the future holds, and though I cannot predict what my successes and failures shall be, I build the Glass House. I can see the home vividly in my mind, and though I know Natalie mustn't meet me, I saw a vision of her in the home on Christmas Eve. $15,128 is enough to house, feed, and bus pass a person for a year, and I've thought to earn that much per focus session twenty to thirty times a year?

My greed and apathy blend me to wish that I can have one solid, true, safe, and real friend. My paranoias tweak and muddle my mind to accuse deceit of some many who are genuinely kind. My faith in God seems awash with notions of understanding premises that are invaluably needed by Christians, yet I don't worship. I wish to give far more than 10% of my money away, yet I've not tithed this year. I can't afford food on my own, yet I lavish in the awareness of my luxuries by having the time, ability, and insight to write books.

Time riddles this world of Earth. So many loves, truths,

passions, and blessings, yet also so many that don't believe they are worthy of water, life, or hope. So many people yearning for their very next breath, yet suffocated with prosperity. Paradoxes of people wishing for money, yet others have spent every fibre of their being living for one that never knew their name.

I hope there always will be tomorrow. "May you always live your next day." While remembering that we're still in today, the day before, some people are living for or in yesterday or the distant past without recognizing that we'll never be there again. We may be trapped in forever, while can recall we're always here now. Perchance we sever from never and crawl into an eternally unfolding moment of how.

I remain faithful, I expect to foster relationships, and I also plan to work bit by bit towards the broader objectives. I release the attachment of 'needing' to achieve them as I've not yet provided homes for people with how I'm living. I seem to know I've not committed to the objective of pushing and marketing Providing Point to other people, and I've been reluctant to sell or promote the idea. I may need to step up and ask more often.

I shall continue to write; I will continue to revise and prepare my books for the market. I also know I'll be content no matter what happens. If I have planted many good seeds, I also must allow them to sprout and grow. Where I've lacked is tending the soil and continuing to plough the fields, yet shall also not forget to tend my garden.

WHAT DID YOU SAY?

Having an idea to choose is much different than following through with a choice. March 17th, 2018, I decided to leave Snowpeaks, though I may return.

I'm a waffle! I've had difficulty making decisions as they float in my mind for a few weeks before deciding. The concern I've had with some choices is how I go back and forth and restructure. That happened with the 100% books to Seed as I made that choice after talking about it a lot for a few weeks and then reverted it in February 2018. Later in *The Sands of Yesterday*, I recommitted 100% of the earnings from individual Fountains to giving.

Such as it is, I chose to scoop from Snowpeaks; a Magic term for conceding. There is absolute freedom by making a choice, yet there also are the insecurities and doubts about consequences and the premise of a 'right' choice. Maybe it's best not to think of the choice as good or bad, or right or wrong, instead, merely that it's a decision made. I chose, I follow through, and I build as best as I can with that choice.

I've had concerns about making decisions because I'm afraid I won't be able to follow up with them. Over the past two weeks, I've been having doubts about my books and creative work and process. I'm concerned about the lack of results of both the book sales and Patreon earnings.

I've been writing about Providing Point since the 4th or 5th Fountains without having yet breached the $50/month goal for pledges. I know that noting my victories and wins is valuable, yet some metrics allude that I've been wasting my time.

Two key people I can remind myself of are my cousin Alex and my friend Kyle. I'm aware they have cared for me exceptionally well, and give me great support, luck, and grace. Kyle's helped me by letting me natter and babble through my insecurities, while Alex allows me to do so too. Vital connections and contacts enable me to a pathway of a more loved and enjoyed future.

We find ways to build and achieve, and with a conversation with Kyle, I committed to three things. One of the choices frightens me. The commitment I made is dual-layered and includes something I've not done so well in the past. I decided to stop smoking inside to adopt a pet.

I've had trepidation about having a pet and not smoking inside because I've been a smoker for twenty plus years and smoked in my apartment. I don't want to smoke indoors and have a pet there because that wouldn't be fair to the animal. I still may smoke cigarettes; just they must be consumed on the patio. I'd like to have a home that is welcoming to non-smokers too. By not smoking inside, it allows me to have more visitors, and it also is a commitment to adopt Zeus, the cat.

Before adopting Zeus, I found it difficult arriving home to an empty apartment and sometimes felt, as mentioned before, very insecure when I got in the door. It had been vacuous when I arrived, and with no pet, girlfriend, or roommate to come home to, it's been a challenge to get grounded and feel safe enough to think.

Two kind and cool friends had just messaged me. Visitors! They were on their way over and linked another critical lesson regarding money and friends. The advice and recommendation are not to leave outstanding balances of things or cash between people. If there is money owed, then repayment can be seen as the reason for contact and not the fact you genuinely like the friend. My Dad and Grandpa advised never to lend and never to borrow; it's a kind reminder of my past errors in judgment.

I feel happy and thankful for the two friends. I'm glad they received the foreign currency I got for them on my trip to Australia, though the outstanding debt with them put a wedge in the way of the friendship was. I feel happy, thankful, and relieved they attended regardless of the outstanding balance and I returned to this book after the visit with them.

We learned a new game; Last Word Theorem. The premise of the game comes from the advice "Be the last one to speak." Being the last one to speak in a group is meant to guide and allow others to share what they have to say without interruption. It makes sure that each person has a chance to speak. The game's challenge is to talk only when everyone else has spoken.

I explained the premise to my visitors, and it resulted in the three friends not saying a word for 15-25 minutes to not 'lose' by speaking first. A result from playing the game led to a parenting idea. If the kids are too vocal, start the game and make sure you also don't say a word. It can lead to some peace and silence.

I found I'm awful at Last Word Theorem. I took the silence of the other three as a chance to play and be a continual 'loser' by speaking. I do get tired of hearing myself talk sometimes, and that may be why I have few friends. Other people too may be tired of hearing me natter on and don't want to contact. A conscious thought, though, in groups to try not to talk until everyone else has spoken, while also remembering to speak up when it's our turn.

Gary reminded me again. I'm not doing the things I need to do to achieve my wishful goals. Even if happiness is a quotient of winning, I'm still not there. Or am I?

I've not put in the massive level of work required for Full Seed; that is clear. With the idea to adjust actions or goals, how do I improve my behaviour? If to level up for my purposes, I don't want to submit and reduce my potential. Three primary things that Gary preaches and teaches are gratitude, empathy, and humility. I feel meek, thankful, and twisted up with sadness, wonder, and whist.

Winning is a kids game, boldly thriving is my objective. I subtly and underwhelmingly know that I'm breaking a lot of the rules and doing irrational and irresponsible things, yet the value I'm searching for with some is different. If I remind the chapter four title, *Let's Be Honest*, what benefits am I seeking and for and from what values?

I'm developing pathways of thought that are muddled, confused, decoded, and then awkwardly presented into books. I'm a sea urchin poking out my notions, fears, and ideas into vacuous wastes of thought to find out if I can achieve an ethical Freedom Solution. I'm displaying the practice of shedding responsibilities and logic while also fusing my authentic thoughts and ideas into genuine appreciation and wonder.

My search is to explore as far into the future as I can while engaging in connection with experiences I have never lived before. Though in a social experiment that we seem to use, my objective is to create intrinsic value through a process of new thought, new idea, and unique experience.

I mix up the thoughts, I assume and consume new premises and theories, and then record it in my subconscious mind through language. I later fuse parts of the ideas with cryptic hints of and for more profound truth.

These books don't make sense to the world at this time. Maybe it's like my music. The linear timelines of spoken speech that then later attach precise meaning that I had zero intent or clues about ever knowing or predicting. Rewind to my job title; Contialitic Shoulsman.

I explained this title as being highly cognitive and sometimes fused to a universal mind. I've also claimed my purpose is to provide, yet my faith and belief tell me that what I produce is who I am and what I deserve.

I present my thoughts and ideas through the written work, and I offer my creations and myself to those who I connect with care. The chance and invested occurrences guide me too as we push towards the edge of time; the last lived moment of existence which we call the present lands us here providing future awareness.

Maybe I'm not meant to afford homes or money. Perhaps I'm just involved with doing what I do, have a bit of fun, and allow the future to unfold into a significant order from what we've done and shall do.

These preceding paragraphs shouldn't even make sense, yet they do. We can, in the present moment, choose to do or say anything we want to. We do have that freedom. We can consciously choose to do anything, though the permanency and long-term consequences are not always predictable.

We each have the power of choice, and our fears of outcome may restrict us from doing things while some others may act impulsively and not consider the effects. Is that a definition of crazy? Doing anything you want to without restriction or fear with pure impulse or automatic responses that are not limited by any means or concern?

Or, is that natural behaviour? Are we following our authentic self in truth, or is that where we are fusing confidence by doing anything, wanting to and hoping to have faith we produce positive results?

If I try to force ideas or lessons on people and I don't know what is best for myself, let alone others, how will I attain the best results? Should I give up on my hopes, goals, and dreams (my future), or should I control how *I* live, think, and behave in the present and shift to full acceptance.

The 7th, 8th, and 9th Fountains are *The Fountains of Fortitude.* We slipped from the word Faith to Fate. Fate may just be accepting whatever happens in the future, though acceptance and choice in the present compared to the faith of imagining something that has not yet occurred.

We can think of language or specific words as temporal and directional links between the tenses of time. The notions of intent as a word and world where we aim to the future and land. What guides the accuracy of our landing?

Acceptance is present based and includes the past from

where we came. If we are warnings, can we also accept our fate and the destiny to think or believe we cannot change a thing? The only actual moment of perception of new life is in the present, yet our past choices guide us in how we experience and behave within them.

If we can become entirely unaware or unconscious of the past, we also can lock ourselves into the present and become aware of bizarrely new things and thought. Because I was in this moment of being 'locked in the present,' I endured and formed these past 600-700 words of text not having a clue as to what I'm even saying.

The thing is, though, these choices from a moment of the present that shall become the past. Since I publish, print, and share these books, the filibuster nonsense of this chapter may still hold some philosophical value. I don't know how these sentences will affect your mind.

Since I don't know how; that's how it's *Open to Fate*. A part of solidified moments of time held from existence into stone from the past. I wasn't there where you are, yet I'll also never be you in the same way you'll never be me. That moment has passed, and then onto the next.

So, yeah, if I shift my attitude and ethics to complete acceptance and also to fate and chance, subtle changes adjust the results. Tampering with the future is maybe a dangerous thing if it's a safety device. If the future is also in my control, I know I also best gain knowledge and not be foolish.

There is value in being honest and accurate, though honesty and sincerity sometimes link these books with what we think of time, effort, and energy. I don't know who's going to read them, yet weak faith calls me to want not to wish.

The value of being exceptionally accepting removes a desire to control, yet maybe it's also a pathway to peace and truth. We may act upon a stationary object, so if we value ourselves not to stay fixed and static, people may not control us. Forward motion.

Moving things is a way we may ward away acts of control, though my obsessive writing and forming of books isn't just a distraction. They are an attempt to remain as a lucid and unattached particle of being and result in developing and sharing ethics and intent.

The intent is often to convey profound ideas, yet I also must pause. When I think another is reading what I'm writing as a projected belief and *not* a communication with the immediate moment of now, how shall they unleash these unexpected results?

I don't want unintentional effects, yet cannot predict the future. I remain accepting of consequences. Who I am, what I do, and the persistence of living long enough to see the future moments allow our results find my process and purpose. It's sometimes more enjoyable when I get to interact with people compared to being solitary though.

My feeling of guilt also compounds. Through the past while, I've been acting freely and seeking happiness and shuffling off responsibility. There are promises I've made that I've yet to fulfill, I've not held stable employment, and authorship hasn't prospered up to now.

With Alpha Games, a local card shop, I'd been spending much time at the shop and hadn't worked on my books or gathered much seed. My guilty feelings stemmed from that. Some think happiness is the primary goal, yet maybe there's truth to that idea too? I love my life, yet note my joy is not perhaps a strong enough purpose for another even if it is a motivation.

I've been vacillating and shifting between ideas and draws of activity and attention. For some months, I obsessively focused on books and the Seed Fund, while at other points, I've focused on relationships and communication. I've been over-focused on earning money, unsuccessfully, and have been prosperous while others have had lack.

I've held faith and hope in my solitary ramblings and ideas, yet my actions have at times been like a teenager. My consistent inconsistency has me concerned because I plant ideas and plans and then fumble into points of wonder. I'm baffled that I've been so oblivious.

I have shown a lack of concern and purpose, and partly, that's why I'm troubled. If I dissect my motivations and thoughts, can I then regather and restore? If I've been active in enjoying life and people, I admit I also have not focused on being engaged with work. I've seen some points of success, just not massive results in the metrics I had set as the goals.

I've been shifting and sliding. It makes me wonder if I'm a snake in the grass that should be concerned society is a mongoose. Maybe a twisted analogy. What have I said? What have I done? The two questions don't line up.

I've said I'll gather for Providing Point, yet instead, I've been providing the points of gathering. I've been interacting with people and being an engaged friend while sluffing off from working and earning for others. I've also, inversely been so focused on work and developing while haven't reached out to connect. I've been too wound up and conscious for my liking.

Some people live their entire lives working just for themselves, and without a family, I may be being too selfish. When I do get to work on these books, then another layer hovers over my being; that I think they are a waste of time.

The opposites of where I believed I would sell thousands of books and house people have shifted to me working on these projects as repentance for living a life I love. Saying I'm repenting for a living I love also calls a strange twist in the question "Why should I feel guilty?"

I answer that question. I've not lived up to my commitments to earning for Providing Point, I haven't been soliciting individuals, companies, and organizations for pledges, and if the books haven't sold and we've found no money, then I must discover a different pathway. If my shift from providing for others has gone back to building my life of happiness, I may need to recalculate.

I haven't yet succeeded in supplying homes, and I've not reached selling books either. We have only eighteen dollars a month pledges to Patreon, and that's an abysmal result of my lack of effort. If nothing matters, though, why be concerned?

Well, I'm concerned, because I know it does matter. I'm going to need some help sorting this out, and I know I cannot do it all on my own. Writing helps me re-centre, yet in which fields shall I put the plow? Who shall work together with me in our shared lives?

THREE THINGS

If we are going to succeed, we must be relevant. With me, it's the Seed Fund, the books, and my life. The Seed Fund is my purpose, yet my life calls for pleasure. I am quite hedonistic, yet compassionate guilt is also a core part of whom I am. If I'm to provide, then I first must earn, though if I am to make money, then how? All the bundles and packets of advice I've seen or read blend into a neurotic self that still is wishing for clarity.

Simplification is helpful. The previous chapter was obtuse and gnarled, and even if holding nuggets of truth, it's difficult to understand. I've wanted to benefit people's lives, and a way to assist is to give advice. Some people, though don't want help.

Some people love being given information, while some others don't yearn for it and won't seek it out. If my books hold good advice, which I'm not clear they do yet, people may want to learn from them and seek them out. If people want to seek them out, then they must be available and in supply. All the layers cross-pollinate as we seed the fields.

My actions of working on my relationship gardens are meant to help the fields. By exposing myself to social situations and being in connection with others, it helps share awareness of who I am too. My skeptical nature about self-promotion trips me up to call my books or music products, yet if I'm going to sell them, then I best call them by the units they are. If I want to earn from my creative work, then books and music are my products.

A twist with Providing Point and business terms shifts differently, as I'm not providing for shareholders. My shareholders are those that are part of my network, yet more specifically the individual community members with whom I wish to serve. That does include friends, yet friends should not be considered customers.

Providing Point's patrons are providers, and providers help provide for people; people that shall use Providing Point's services. My sporadic and inconsistent behaviours may be an asset to the process, yet by being fragmented and scattered through many different groups, points of time, and contacts do we gain a more extensive web of exposure?

I centred on helping Alpha Games with their card sorting for a few weeks. Some of the dregs, a term used by the owner of the shop, include a few who've processed some of my creative works. Selling my cards to Alpha Games also helped me order copies of books to share, which are a step forward.

The impulse to share the books is sometimes congruent with the recommendations of others to pursue my dreams and not give up. For the 4th Fountain copies ordered into town, they sell for $10 each with $5 to Providing Point and $5 to cover the cost of ordering them. From the copies of the March 21st batch, $97.20 went to Providing Point for sharing locally. This money was the first money that Providing Point shared in 2018.

Though my Dad doesn't like the idea of me ordering books, the urgency of providing is evident and selling books is a pathway towards doing so. It's not only my Dad that assures me I need to care for myself first before helping others. I must insist that I'm doing this to care for me too.

I evade saying some things because of fear of judgment from my Dad, and I shall attempt to justify them. That may be the rationalization I wish not to make. Because my Dad values self-responsibility and not so much sharing with strangers, I may be foolish to tell you these things. My lax actions for Providing Point show how I don't like pursuing the cause monetarily; I don't like asking for money.

I had an intake for volunteering at Ruth and Naomi's, a street-level mission for those in need, and that's a way to give too. I need more community involvement, and it seems I have my fingers in a few different pies. I quit SnowPeaks in March and have sometimes wondered about my writing. My reasons come from different motivations, though it's true the separate ideas, commitments, and activities can blend for multi-win ideas.

If the books don't sell, does that mean we can't reach Full Seed? If the books sell, how can we confirm the idea of Providing Point is a good one? If we sell books, then we can share the thoughts and intents of the Seed Fund and garner more support, yet is the program the right thing?

The Fountains books are part of the Patreon rewards, and as people start to read the books, the incentive of purchasing copies can potentially increase patronship. The more patrons we have, the more we can give and share with Providing Point, therefore having a more significant impact, and the more effect Providing Point has, the more relevant the books can be. By being inclusive and more relevant, we can gather more people to work together.

Dad, you know that I've been persistent, and I know I have been foolish and obsessive. My books haven't yet sold, and I have bought copies to bring into Chilliwack. Having books to sell can earn money too, and the February inversion of Patreon and Amazon sales commitments can assure a positive result. My firm belief is that by working for others *and* Providing Point can and shall guarantee an income source for me too.

My work in Chilliwack finds three things; we learn to live, earn to give, and mere wishes are filtered out by the sieve.

As the Fountains have developed, I dabble in separate waters gathering the components, and though my scattered behaviours and thoughts allow the streams to form, we glean the streams of life, energy, and also income.

At Alpha Games, I tended some personal emotional and social needs, and I earned some survival money by selling Magic cards. I'd gotten to share my music, books, and codes with people, and I was allowed to help a liked and appreciated business owner with his shop. The benefit of gathering with various people helps shape the fabric of my creative work, and it's rad to be part of a life where our presence is valued and trusted. I don't always feel welcome, though, and wonder if I'm pushing my luck.

Ruth and Naomi's hadn't brought me on, though I still tend my needs to interact, understand, and meet people. As an extension of my work, goals, and objectives, it's best to know the people whom which Providing Point intends to help though. Relationships are a fundamental human need, and functionally, I like to know how and what I can do for others.

And Toastmasters? I chose the pathway of Team Collaboration. Toastmasters can help me learn how and where to share the large-scale ideas to a real-life audience. The response from the February 22nd speech reminds me that people do care about the homeless situation and that an honest call for compassion may help if I can learn how to communicate the program; especially to those who can afford to provide monetary support. Learning how to speak to an audience will not only help clarify how to present the value proposition of contributing to help those in need, though also can expand the reach of our ideas.

I note another nuance here. In a meeting with Graham from Chilliwack Health and Housing, he noticed how I use the term 'we' when I was referring to Providing Point. Technically he's right, I was only one person working back then, and that I referred to what 'we' have done and are going to do. This work as a combined effort and not just myself, we just haven't yet gathered all the team and components.

I've used the term *we* like this a common cause and not me alone. If people don't ally, maybe it is just my books and

I. If people buy the Fountains, though, they are contributing, and as others join to provide through Patreon, they are part of the 'we' also. Providing Point is not me attempting to be a saviour or messiah; it's a gathering of people together to help a humanitarian cause in our local community.

In recent months I've been very narrowly focused on my wants and not thinking so much of those in need. I have levelled up my thoughts and integration, though it's only here again I get outside the halls of my mind and outwards to other countries and worlds.

I'm condensed into a singular nodal point, and still, thankfully, my intents start to breach out past the narrow confines of my mind. Thank You! Three in one is another allusion to how God works through us each as individuals. I thank Him for that reminder and send a wish and prayer He continues to guide me and my comprehension.

This chapter turned out to be a super short section, though, because the energy shifted. We cross into a new path.

ROBERT KOYICH

RESET THE FOUNDATIONS

I've felt like I'm wasting my life. I've not accomplished much, even if some may say I wrote a few books up to now. I haven't found a girlfriend, I've not had regular employment, and I've not secured a path of profitable authorship. A dear friend had called me back from earlier in the day, though, reminding me to be positive.

The disparaging pushes and pulls find me wanting to bitch and complain about my life when there is a lot of good. There are the ideas to work and earn a living, and I do have a home to live in. There are ever repeating patterns of feeling awful, not having much, and then diving into a pot of coffee writing books, yet I also now have my cat, a bit of food, tobacco, and, sometimes, hope.

I would like to earn my living yet still show the gravity of not, however, finding a definite and pure purpose. My cigarettes are a distraction, the coffee seems to be my drug of choice, and then I remember I can write anything. I have obsessed about the Fountains and have an idea they may matter.

Though, even if I can write valuable ideas and premises that could change the fabric of decency into ordinary cloth, what does it matter if no one wears it? People know I've been weaving tapestries, yet the walls of my soul here are bare. My

41

impulsive urges sometimes have called me to self-destruct and shred paintings like a lucid artist.

I climbed high and hopeful thinking of my dream girl; then reality pushed me back down the slide to the bottom of never. Not forever as I thought it was, yet still the ever-constant awareness that I'm here and haven't accomplished much. I was two cups of coffee into these pages knowing I committed to six hours of wakefulness at 9:42 PM. When I did so, I got excited about writing and said: "committed to the process" like a declaration of worth, and then, shouted like a person about to be locked up in the psych ward.

The three weeks before I had been smoking inside, though a choice to smoke on the patio instead came from the idea to adopt a cat. If Zeus lives in my home, I must not smoke inside. I had also acquired another buffer for my being in May 2018; I now have a TV and Netflix at home.

I watched a documentary about the spacecraft Voyager, and it cued vague ideas of what was happening when my parents conceived me. The notion that people use rockets as a metaphor for ejaculation made me wonder if my parents conceived me at the point of Voyager 1 or Voyager 2 in 1977. I was born in May 1978.

The Voyager spacecraft left Earth to view the other planets in our solar system. When I saw the first recorded images of Jupiter, they seemed like a hallucination and painted deceit of there really being another planet. The flat Earth people have nothing on the premise that all is a mere figment of our imagination, though. Those that believe nothing outside of themselves exists are called solipsistic.

My imagination also has fooled me to believe that everything outside of my consciousness is a delusion. I've even thought that everything I perceive is a direct and immediate sign relevant to me. I've held these beliefs semi-frequently when writing, yet my desire for financial results requires there to be others to process what I have formed. My awareness of having achieved little through my work, though, shows support for the delusion.

In moments of solitary awareness, inceptive messages, emails, and 'bling's from the phone surgically incept my consciousness with deft synchronicity, and these sounds from my phone seem to incept ideas and awareness into my mind surgically. Spinning to psychic impressions, I can sometimes anticipate these sounds before they occur; however, I cannot predict the future.

The people that can plan months or years into the future successfully hold a high power that I lack at this point. The persistence of keeping pressing the keys and slugging the cursor across the page with woven ideas is a skill, yet how will it be appreciated if there's no one to perceive it?

My wants still are few, and I have been setting a few goals to give myself something to work towards with life. With sorting cards at Alpha, I could earn some money, yet purchasing cards was a lure too. I wanted to invest and buy and sell Magic cards again, yet it's a dangerous lure to chase a return. A strong urge of profit can draw action, though, and those that want to earn money can find ways to do so. The thirst, though, for money concerns me.

With my books, they also seem to tip me forward to spill a drink. I've wanted to order printed copies to sell books, yet when I get money focused and profit-driven, I seem to stifle myself. Some people may want money, go out and earn it, and then revel in having massive or comfortable amounts of income. That's one way to prosperity. I'd also like to make ethical earnings and not through coerced sales or forced labour.

Someone buying a copy of my book is, in some cases, a gift of them sharing love or appreciation. Oppositely, I like to share gifts with others to show my love or appreciation. It's true that some sales and Providing Point earnings may come from sharing the books. Relaying copies of my work to earn money may draw awareness from authentic care and legitimate interest if to succeed.

Those who read the books may glean compassion and share the causes mentioned in the books, and others may find interest in understanding them through reader recommendations. *The Fountains of Fortitude* have shown that my wishes were the sand I was building on, yet I fell back into realizing that only a rare few care about my hopes, goals, and dreams.

Just like me, some people want sure things and not whimsical fancy. I may have gone into the oceans from the salty shoreline, yet it's more explicit that I've found I don't want to only sit on the beach. I desire a life amongst the other wildlife and not to sit at home and burn. Trepidation dissipates, and I pray we find prosperity.

And yet still, a teetering nervousness holds an edge. Coffee is substantially an issue for me. The late nights I've spent working in the fields of text are my responsibility as well as tending the soil on public grounds. My work is like a commune, and that word links to an idea from January 2018. When I was visiting my Dad then, he commented that he thinks I'm more of a socialist than he is. That statement is true, yet let me extrapolate.

I believe in a universal basic living income. Income need not be a wage, yet the majority of the population believes that people should have a job. An Italian saying is *chi non lavora, non mangia*. The translation is 'Who does not work does not eat.' If that is true, then I hope to work to earn for others to eat.

My Dad thinks me socialistic, yet I know I'm positively money focused sometimes. I thought of two terms; calling someone a social capitalist or a capitalizing socialist. I can be the social capitalist working and earning money for myself and others and then provide for those so we all can have good things. I also don't want to a capitalizing socialist grabbing at free things without earning them.

The premise of meritocracy is right; I must work to earn my money and not mooch. I also have empathy for those without and wish my books may be a conduit for providing and receiving. I know I don't have massive amounts of income for myself, yet an abundance of resources would be grand.

If I earn excess, I don't see it as an obligation to share; it's reciprocation. Giving in the future is partly because of my gratitude for being allowed the life I live now. I am not entitled to what I have, yet am profoundly thankful to have such. I use my ability to give because of gladness, and yes, a bit of guilt. Appreciation of having things is a motivation to give to others; especially those for whom we have compassion or care.

When Providing Point reaches $50 pledged per month, the first five Share and Care cards will be in circulation. I know who the first five recipients are, yet from previous experience realize I should not write their names in this book. As there is only $18/month pledged at this point, I remember I have made grand promises previously and then hadn't been able to maintain them.

Though I've made audacious claims and goals that I haven't yet reached, I also press on and endure. A conversation with a friend almost had me entirely give up on the books and Providing Point on March 29th, 2018. The friend gave me lots of input and advice, and a lot of what he said holds merit and value. From the conversation with him, I mutated the help and guidance while blending wisdom.

I shall not give up on the books or Providing Point; I do, though, need to form some repentance from my bold wishes and proclamations. I keep creating the books and releasing them, though the most important take away from the conversation with the friend might be to release the attachment to rely on the financial gain from authorship. I don't need to stop writing or working; I need to release my obsession of needing to earn from my book work.

If I can create for value and interest, release my projected expectation or need of a monetary return from my authorship, regather, and then honestly care and tend people with love, perhaps we do find an alternate form of a mutually positive future.

I started writing another project during the formation of the base of this chapter. The text is called *Nodal Input* and launched from a conversation with a dear friend. The premise of the document is to share my Magic codes and language openly. *Nodal Input* includes the Mox code, Planeswalker referencing, and my understanding of social parameters based on mathematics and perception. Colour referencing and group dynamics are part of the systems, and there also is some personality theory and explanation.

The audience base for *Nodal Input* is exceptionally narrow, yet I would like to share the concepts. The friends I labelled Planeswalkers help me hone in on truth and are beneficial for my understanding and trust. I'm thankful that our subvert understanding clarifies and reveals the multiple attempts of deception and abuse.

With mental stimulation, a conversation can be an involved and substantial thing. If we combine the idea of block-chain technology, think of each friend as having a database of ourselves and all they remember of us. There are different data points and input; what they hear, what we've typed, what visual memories or impressions of us they have.

Some friends also know how we feel, smell, and in rare cases, how we taste. If each person is a separate database of our input, then think of the networking capabilities and cross-referencing when we bond. With myself, my books, codes, and music, there are multiple base points of 'me' in the world.

My recordings are theoretically the same base set of input and the books all cement as solidified works. The threads of codes, contact, and connection weave in the music and books, yet the individual people who've heard or read them are processing centres of their own.

The way I feel and perceive others may not convey accurately. Many could presume what they think from their own belief, yet mental deception is a real thing. We all don't know the abuse or challenges others have gone through that make them who they are. There is a core of who we are and how we exist that is theoretically never understood entirely by anyone else. What about the premise of God though?

The idea of universal omniscience is a different way to think of God. Linked to a previous Fountain's ideas of G.O.D. as being the Global Organized Directive or the Galactic

Organizing Directive, compound the concept of God as knowing absolutely everything. Galactic Omniscient Deity.

Consider that every letter of this book, and other publications, has been explicitly compiled without consent from the authors. I may think I have written my books, yet the surgical implants of inceptive editing, the points in time when we read, and the consequences of what happens if and when the information processes are beyond my control.

The two words *fate* and *destiny* also hold different connotations. We can consider fate as an outcome that was meant to happen. Destiny can be a wish for future events to pass and become reality, and once happening can be considered fate. It was fate that we met on a plane of existence that holds more than just Earth. It was destiny that allowed the moment of the present to unfold. Let the bold choice enable us to wade amongst the sunsets.

Each grain of sand holds a crystalline structure moulding form and positions as a static point and place of time and space. Every moment we experience is now, and all that happened is the fate foretold that we can recall in the present. Anything you remember in the future is destiny unfolded, even if you may or may not have wished for it. Every event of the past must have occurred to allow the moments you become aware of to be.

Destiny has not yet told me that the *Key to Me* is something worthwhile to add to the hands of eternity. I form the warm drink to link the swarm of ink into the pink lighter's ignition. Wishing upon a star that she precisely knows who you are.

We all can make choices. Free will is a thing. The trip, though, is that no matter what we do, we move into new moments of time. It cannot be any different than it is according to the parameters of what happened before to allow us to choose moments of rhyme.

Our path may be narrowly affecting and redirecting all the other timelines; from their placement next to ourselves and our actions. We can divert a linear or direct approach, yet twine back to the premise of linear time theory in that all things are unidirectional. We can't reverse real life, yet we can modify the consequences. It's a trip, and one I wish not to leave.

SIGNS FROM THE UNIVERSE

Am I devoted to the cause or a stubborn mule? Hold the fabric of time with the dramatic climb down with truth and love. With the rhymes below the dove starts to flow. Set the net to abet the Jet and remind the merchant that Gary's nowhere near done yet.

The sun began to rise again when the lies found the pad and pen. Pressing the keys to the lion's den, a hen calls the cow back to the plow, and to quote Toby Keith "How do you like me now?"

Green mana was meant to become legal in July. People, now, can legally smoke marijuana in Canada. I'm still not able to do so! I'd love to smoke pot again, though I also know the consequences; hospital, insanity, and restrictive poverty. Understanding the implications of how marijuana is for me keep me from doing so. There also is paranoia and a near inability to talk, though that's bundled in with the insanity.

Blue mana can be tears, meth, and water. Intellect and deceit are not kind, yet sometimes vital for survival. I know I'm not a general and don't want to command troops, yet it seems that the war is going on. Even with subvert ideas that I shouldn't know, I'm thankful for the Apple links.

I'm grateful for Dad and Sarah and glad that I have books to form and read. There may be a substantial benefit by returning to reading to learn and expand. It's also an investment to make more time for language learning.

Red mana links to primary, visual, and battling people. Rubies are passionate, though I shall not lose the fire. We cultivate my passions and desires to thrive, while the Ruby Loverock and Primary Lovestone hold the node. It's best we also fuse allegiance and honour to the Sprites. Mox Opal linked in with Jeskai as the lasers blast out the grout. Arigato!

White mana links to forces, instincts, and systems. A Bant nodal point (green, white, blue) conducts a single node in the Contialis with an adept reach like an urchin. Some carry the sequences and series digitally, and as we evolve, adaptation becomes valuable. My books and work may not make sense though.

In many things, the ideas of religious unity, the worlds of nature and technology, and the shoulic blend of all people and language are also nodal points. Mooshka may deepen mental stability and is part of future Fountains.

Black mana twists the ciggies, sound, and life. The Selesnya node to Grixis holds relative lines to an Emerald, yet if we add to the meld, past crewmates and also foundational seed people like Jon blend. Dual lands and planeswalkers light up the smoking and find the reasons as to why I consume.

I was getting closer to tossing away the habit and addiction, and it fell back in strong upon returning from Australia. My home smelled pretty atrocious from smoking inside, yet I don't forget the outer space links from Jet associations.

I started another document in April 2018. The material is called *Nodal Input* and covers the Magic ideas and codes plus Shoulspeak. I may not make the document public because I don't know what value the book holds for another to read. I'd like to form and complete *Nodal Input*, though the audience is for Magic friends and primary contacts. *Fragments of Intent* also needed revision when I wrote this.

A few people have told me I should shift genres or even the medium that I've been using. Diamond recommended visual art, and Opal also told me to take up pottery. Why would I shift to entirely unknown art forms if the objective is to hone existing skills and form a creative profession? Is it me resisting a different path, or mastering a different way of writing?

Considering how many people have read my books, I'm not clear that there's a large enough sample base to deem the books market worthy or not. Opal had asked me about my marketing plan. Bizarrely I could articulate my current project, yet I still carried the agitation at the results shown up to that point. Opal told me "You're twitching." That may be a sign I'm still over-obsessed, and my defiance of adjusting my medium may need re-evaluation.

Profound layers of poor choices seem to fuse into the meld. Thankfully, I'm living on Earth, even if another human thought I'm of otherworldly birth. Maybe I should shift to baffling linguistics and compound the parameters that explain the confusion. If I can form or decipher a long string of information, is it dangerous to convert it into plainly understandable English?

What would happen if I tried to infuse and mix with false ideas, premises, and theories? I honestly would prefer to help enlighten people to the truth, though what if I've been misinformed and misguided; even if unintentionally? Does that mean I should put the keys away and learn to pray, even if in a non-religious and secular way?

If the crucial pieces of information are mentally leaked when I write and form these books, does that explain how they have a function cognitively and telepathically? Even if no one else reads them, I'm attempting to gather and guide. I'd like to provide, and don't want to mooch or borrow time, money, or grace. If I am meant to be alone and isolated, I'm still delighted, fortunate, and grateful to interact with the rare few humans that talk to me.

I've gone through possession before, and I've written previously about how I used to transform into other people and feel like I was entirely them. I'm also now wondering of outer space and if my delusional beliefs are fusing elements of the cosmos that are meant to be secret.

I know how I'm only one entity and explicitly not in a dream world, yet the beliefs of others would skew and twist my mind into believing their truths instead of the core of who I am. Do you note how you can't openly express to another your core truths sometimes?

How are these the *Fountains of Fortitude*? They have drawn delusion, fantasy, and utterly illogical thought and sequences of words from my keyboard. How can there be fortitude with such obscure ideas as the foundation to hold them? Building a house upon sand is awful. What if I've been creating my universe upon illusions that would make sand seem surer than a titanium base?

I saw the movie *The Infinity Wars* the day I wrote this. It was strange. There were moments in the movie theatre that I'd seen from dreams much time before seeing the film in real life. Another friend a few days prior told me also of how they don't know when they're in waking life or in dreams. When they don't know if they're awake or dreaming, they can perform actions to decipher if awake and in reality.

I almost always understand when I'm awake or dreaming. More lucidly I remember when I'm awake and have imagined something before. Imagination can take us to exceptionally fanciful points of life, and some online mentors and life coaches recommend visualization to activate our minds; to create the experiences we want.

If fear is the guiding energy or thought, though, I warn you not to accept your believed fate. Hope, faith, and belief are positive when coupled together, yet I intuit that fear, confidence, and uncertainty can be potently dangerous too. When a person's energy shifts to a negative place, it's even more crucial to slow down, breath, and reassess.

What am I trying to achieve? I had focused on Natalie, success, and the Seed Fund, yet the results up to when I wrote this seemed to call for me to instead go down a path of destruction. I put alcohol in my tea when I wrote this, and I must not corrupt the energy of this work. Weirdly, my cigarettes call me back to a neutral balance as I paused to get a cup of water instead. I shifted from sadness as the first emotion and attempt to settle into a reset point.

The process of forming this text reminds me we need other people as a groundwire for ourselves. We need an outlet for our negative or potential negative energy to dissipate it from our souls. Not our spirits; those, I hope and pray, are unchangeable and hold the vital data of who we indeed are.

Our minds are not ours alone to own. The potential of other people's thoughts or actions to change the ideas that reside in our consciousness hold power if we shall produce good or bad. A pure spirit can change the fabric of the mind with inceptive contact.

Heed your intuition. You know yourself better than I, or anyone else, and can tell who you are and how you feel. People may attempt to change your actions and beliefs, yet cross-reference them with your truths and awareness. Do not believe everything everyone tells you. Do not find everything you think.

Some may be lying or acting on false information and being knowledgeable about your real truths. Preserving the core is vital. Voicing your truths may be necessary to regain and hold your integrity, so when you grasp hold of yourself and become stable, it's the time to assert what's in line and accord with you universal purpose, function, and truth.

Do you hear voices? I don't mean the sounds of others that are real audible spoken words in the space you are within; I mean the inner nudges and inklings of truth or even the bossy commanding voices that tell you what to do.

Some people know of their conscience and the guiding recommendations that say "don't do that" or "do it." Some other people have ultra-negative commands that could lead to or from insanity. Oppositely some may have voices they hear in their mind that are of loved ones that passed away.

When I was in college, I wrote a paper about if we can know another's mind. My argument was that we could never comprehend all of our own thoughts, so how can we ever know entirely what another's mind is. What I want to dredge is my self-awareness so that I can have an entire understanding of my being. I'd like to know and comprehend myself so well that I can know explicitly what is me, what is not, and then tell another.

I was diagnosed as a paranoid delusional schizophrenic, though my recent diagnosis is an undifferentiated schizophrenic. I have difficulty, sometimes, knowing what is other and what is me. Some people believe that every thought we hear in our mind is only our own, though I don't hold that belief. I believe in telepathy and crossed views, and if the premises of God by any religion infuse, then we know it's not all ourselves that created the world.

Some people posit that each of us is God, yet I don't agree with that. I know I'm not omniscient and ascribe that quality to the Global or Galactic Organized Directive. In a universal consciousness theory, God knows *all* things. How does that apply to something that is entirely unknown? Theoretically, there may be something that is entirely isolated and not in the conscious knowledge of any living or non-living being.

Omniscience would know of the uknown too. With humans, we don't do some things in *any* of our conscious minds as there are still things not yet discovered or created. The premise of omniscience is that those things *are* known; *all* things. All things include the consciousness of other animals and plant life too.

I am not omniscient. Of the knowledge pool of Earth, I barely know anything. I'm just one single node in the Contialis. I may have a vast amount of self-derived notions and thoughts unique and personal to myself, yet outside of myself, I know so very little.

I don't even know many mainstream pop-culture references that are substantially common knowledge to many people. I may be an obscure reference point that few know of, yet as people come to know me, my work, and my ideas, a diffusion of my being seeped out into the world. I must assure, by my responsibility to Earth, the cosmos, and time, that what I create is beneficial.

Or is it best I remain obscure and unknown? Is what I write vital? For many, no. That may be why many people haven't understood me. We can't force the rest of the world to follow ethical principles, and I don't know what the best thing or right thing is to do for the globe. I don't even comprehend what is best for myself.

It is a responsibility to tend to the world, yet I still lack wisdom and acceptance. From a thought in my mind when forming books a few months ago, I was told that I have no control over even the sequence of words I use, let alone their results.

Free will is a luxury some have, yet I'm desperately wishing I can channel into correct patterns and activities. I don't have free reign to do what I want to do. I also have lacked faith that I'll make the right choices. My hedonistic pleasures and desires could take me to destruction, and I don't want to rely so heavily on grace and forgiveness.

The miraculous happenstances of chance and fate have served me well up to now, so to the Higher Powers, I pay homage. Mia amica contialitica, siamo entrambe pazzi. You know you, and I forever will think I have.

12:36 AM, May 2nd, 2018

Forty years on this planet. I still like how I know it's a riddle that's played me into solidarity with nothing. I souled my soul to the treble, yet the pebbles of sand remind that sandals must stand. We are grains on the shoreline of rhyme.

In time, we climb into the view of how I wish you knew that I thought I had a clue. It may be the technology that made me obsess of you, Nat, yet a lie it may be to say I ever see.

As a close to this chapter, without claiming any religious terms or deities as truth or fact, I send out a secular prayer as a wish to skip across the pond. Though it's not yet dawned on the day, let me learn to thrive so well I can create the ways to say I can never stay a day away. When the voice chooses to make my heart pray, it started with play. I look into the world to find some things discretely and inwardly curled. I'm thankful that the years have unfurled.

Thank you, God, for letting me live. Thank you, Mom and Dad, for giving me birth and life. Thank you to the friends, family, and community that allow me to live this way. I ask all of you that my life isn't even halfway done.

Merci to the forces that be, and for eternity holds the key; I can never claim that any of the strength of the world is under the control of me and what I wish to be.

Let our lives be free to assure we see the ocean meets the Sea. Amen.

A NEED TO CHOOSE

During the three weeks between when I wrote the previous chapter and this one, I'd not felt so well. I've been riddled with insecurities, apathy, and doubt, yet still am thankful to be alive. I spoke with Chandra earlier in the day and told her how I feel I lack purpose and motivation.

My sleep had been erratic with wake up times in the afternoon most days, and I didn't feel inspired. My belief in the bookwork had been near nil, and I wonder again if I'm not persevering, yet instead delusional. The nagging feeling somewhere in my body, though, fuels the obsession to create even though it's not rational.

Regarding the premise of value not always being a monetary thing, I still felt poor. I don't think I've built books or work that will form a legacy, and it's instead felt like I'm selfishly and bullishly shaping books with no substantial purpose.

This section may seem to be like a pity party, and I don't mean to be a Debbie Downer. I also write, sometimes, to run the feelings through my being as an attempt to cleanse and refresh my mind and attitude.

I've thought my life and words are being corralled and channelled into pathways not all my own. Religious tones of thought seep into my concerns attempting to give me hope and faith. If all things are destined to occur, then does that mean I have zero choices in the matter? I may need to be patient to allow the course of events. The precise results of my efforts are what drove me into the feelings of hopelessness, and my wishful mind tries to counteract those feelings by giving me the idea I have a purpose.

When I think or judge what I'm creating isn't going to be processed, that's what's made me feel I've wasted my efforts. For my work, and most of my life, I've thought I'm smart, yet I also could accurately be called stupid or a fool.

When I try to force or push to have a knowledge-based purpose, there is a want to tell you recommendations about how to improve your life. If my life is not in order or thriving, though, how could the advice I give help you? It may because your life is not my life and your outlook and mindset may be in a more positive state.

You may be open to gleaning insight and activating the lessons I've not been able to use correctly in my life, and perhaps I should go back to some foundational blocks and intents; to make a restatement of what my wants and objectives are. These statements also must be honest and real, and not what I think I *should* do, though what I genuinely desire.

I want to continue living. I want to engage in more human interaction. I would like to remove some of my self-defeating behaviours, though honestly, I also don't want to quit smoking or stop writing and shaping these books. I want to have fantastic results from my writing while not needing to focus or think about marketing or sales, and that statement, to me, could be said as "I want the results, yet not have to put in the effort."

Up to now, the natural course of events have had me write a lot, and I should note that too. I *have* written a few books, and they *are* an accomplishment. My attachment to financial results, or rather the lack of them, is what's troubled me. I've been hooked up on wanting to share the books, though don't know how they benefit another. They have been very self-focused, and I don't think the Fountains are relaying a solid value proposition to potential readers.

This section reminds me that I've been too focused on what I want. I think I need to focus more on what other people want, or rather yet, what I can do for other people that will benefit them.

Secondary gains are an idea I've had. The notion of secondary gains is supplying or providing for others and then receiving the secondary benefits from my right and just actions. If my Mom used to tell me "behaviours have consequences" it may be time to adjust my behaviours again.

What do I do that helps or improves the lives of another? The first answer I have to that question is "be their friend." If I'm over-focused on my work and isolated at home in the middle of the night working on books, that may not be a win for anyone. If only a few read the books I write, could that still be a benefit?

I need to be cautious of interacting with people that have an intent to hurt me too. My neurotic twist wonders if I've been reacting because I've had negative thoughts and have been thinking about how others can benefit me. I have, at times, been selfish, greedy, and have had a lack of compassion or decency. I need to adjust how I've been behaving and what I've allowed in my mind.

My financial lack has been a factor, yet that's also my responsibility. I haven't been working a job, my books haven't sold, and I've not made positive reciprocal relationships that remember the premise of win/win. I have been thinking about my gains without thinking about what I can do to improve situations with a bit of love and care.

There was a focal point in my heart the morning I wrote this. I felt some of the most profound sadness I've felt in the past three to four years when working on the book *Etched in Stone*. Since I've never met Natalie and had a conversation, the ideas and delusions fortify in my awareness as something I can't prove or entirely denounce. I remind us all that I cannot ever claim that it's the Imbruglia Natalie because who I've felt in my soul and spirit may not be the famous singer.

It's like I'm a boat travelling down the river that is attached to a pier, and what I really should understand is the depths of how much I can care, and not attribute the feelings to a specific person. I honestly don't know who Natalie is, and it's compounded further by the question: "How could she ever know who I am if she's never spoken to me either?"

So wishes and fortitude remove the fantasy and reset the lure that they use. A fusion reaction of stellar natural attraction nearly put me in traction for thinking of love. I cannot claim who the dove shall dwell with, yet the Ith holds the myth of what she believes in the weaves of text in communities and consects.

What times have her and I even had? Is there even one moment of life that she has experienced me? The tree of self revives the shade that lets the Spirit wade in the drink of what we think. I wonder if I should write to my future five-year me again like how I wrote in *Seeds of Tomorrow* a chapter of my five-year future self; back to the moment of then.

Maybe I need to write to the energy and spirit that I sense as Natalie and make sure that Nat is a lie. Perhaps Coleman is right, and the real love that cares for me as much as I had Nat is out there on Earth wishing me to know her real name. Have I mislabeled the spirit in my heart?

What happened to Demma? We were a real love. I liked her a lot, though is she still sad or angry I didn't keep in contact. She was a remarkable, vibrant, and beautiful, yet I've not thought of her often or as strongly as True. I remember how I loved life when Demma and I were together. We were happy and had fun while Natalie has sometimes been sadness and despair. The keys speak to me through the words I see. She said "no," yet I don't know which one mentioned it.

I've felt riddled with doubt in my isolation. I could call out and ask the ones I love about who my lovestone is, yet I'm sure they don't know either. I don't understand how it is to live together. I clear the webs of deceit and how they want me beat, yet the laced treat holds the breath that keeps seeping tea into how I don't know who's for me.

In the keys, the next day, my awareness shifted to how I need to plan for the future, and not just a relationship. I need to know how I'll earn money to afford to live the life I desire. With the results yet shown from working on books, I'm not sure authorship shall be profitable; it certainly hadn't seemed that way up to August 2018.

My concerns heed me that buying and selling Magic cards is potentially a money and greed path for me. Writing books may not yet have been an income source, yet their social value is higher than only focusing on money. Books can help other's lives too; they hold more purpose than just a monetary quotient.

We see reading this that my love life is a concern, my financial lack is bright, though socially I've also had issues. It's seemed that I'm a focus of conspiracies and negative attention, and because of how insecure I feel out and about, I'm inclined to stay home at the plow; working on the books. A strong intuition tells me to do that since I'm not working full-time.

Some seem to be upset at me. When I was at the welfare office, I seemed to sense there are plots and plans of which I'm the focus. My fears of critical power and attention must not overwhelm me, and maybe it's a good choice to be a home-bound soul instead of pushing myself out into the community. Each of us must make decisions about how we shall live, and when I fear the criminal activities and energy towards myself, I seem to neglect how love and life may be gathered and built.

I know I can't please everyone, yet my desire to be alive and do something worthwhile calls me out into the world. I thought to make a book of thanks to people I knew before Chilliwack. I'd like to acknowledge my appreciation to my past, though I might neglect to mention some names or people. There are needs to choose, though.

Each of our lives is the consequence of a series of choices of both our own and others. Our attitudes source from how we've responded to those choices, and it's nice to think we can choose how we live our lives. Our consequence of actions is also a valid thing and decisions about how we live to affect our current day realities.

I don't have a car because I don't work full-time to afford one. I don't have a girlfriend or a regular friend group in my home because I've not sought out or tended relationships very well. I've been a smoker for 24-25 years, and I remind myself that it's a choice too. I have often chosen pleasure and self-gratification over long-term planning and the requirements to lead a long, healthy life.

My decision to avoid some things may not resolve issues, so words must be processed to allow stability. I can tend to and work towards correcting my behaviours, and my choice to not smoke marijuana or other drugs keeps me closer to sanity and out of the psych ward. My decision to join and stay with Toastmasters allows me skills and confidence to speak to people.

My opportunity to write allows clarity and a potential pathway to shared prosperity and success. I choose to curtail some things, yet feel the opposite pull of wanting to dive deep into coffee and all-night writing sessions. Instinctively I adapt and make the right decisions.

Another weird set of choices I make is which words to type or how I edit and distribute the books. When anyone reads one of my printed books, you see a linear sequence of text I've adapted and modified. There are multiple versions of the Fountains, and though the ideas are similar, subtle and significant grammatical and contextual corrections develop.

A book is a congruent exposition of a series of choices, and my determination to form them solitarily also is a decision I've yet to comprehend. I do have limitations and restrictions while the Law of Attraction and Success Coaches advocate we can do anything we want. They also tell us we can achieve any goals we set. It's encouraging to believe that, and be rational.

Where we are and what we hold as a start point is different for each. As you see with me, I have decades of poor choices and actions that I need to rectify, so I shall. It's a conscious effort and commitment to be determined to adjust some of the things I do.

I'm open to receiving miracles, blessings, and peace. We can choose love over anything, and if you do, I hope you add respect and unity too. Think of where you are now, yet don't always think of where you need and want to go. Think also of what is pleasant for you in your current situation and gather more of that.

I love being at home with friends and also working on productive books. If I allow myself to do so, I can keep my heart, mind, and soul in the plow and keep open to connections with people. I cannot plow my love in other people's gardens, though. I can, admittedly, cultivate a pleasant and beautiful garden and find others that want to develop, grow, and build with me from a central point at home.

Maybe it's best I don't go out trying to plow the fields. If others can do that far better than I can, perhaps I can give them some good seeds.

FRACTIONALIZED REALITY

(This section is from a thought experiment cued by Christy Whitman as a response to a question about Heaven on Earth; before and after I watched her video)

Before the video:

I'm not clear that I understand Heaven. I cognitively get that people can live in enlightened heavenly states while alive as humans on Earth, yet I also think globally. Religious contexts guide me to recall those that have passed on, and I remember Christy's QSCA (Quantum Success Coaching Academy) show; she had an episode with a medium named James Van Praagh. James communicates with those passed on.

I don't understand the afterlife and don't think of the dead often in my conscious mind. I do, though, have belief in spirits and invisible energies, entities, and actions. I believe there are spiritual realms that crossover here on Earth, yet the cliché view of a Utopian society being Heaven is a notion. The world of dreams also have had me in a few reincarnation scenarios I've dreamt, and I'm not clear yet about nirvana and non-living realms.

I'm an incredibly immediate reality person. What I mean

by that is that I'm almost always neurotically conscious of being in the present. I rarely think of the past and am not so often envisioning the future. If I slow down and process the question: "do you think creating Heaven on Earth is possible?" I'm inclined to suggest that Heaven is unique for each person. We each can have our own personal Heavens, Hells, and Purgatories.

In the moment of forming this, I chose to work towards my future, yet that is extended life on Earth. I don't want to go to Heaven in the real world because I don't want to die to get there. I have, in my waking Earth life, seen multiple points of where Heaven exists on Earth and believe in perfect moments in our lives. We are allowed heavenly moments; moments of peace, and love, and togetherness. I don't want to die to leave people behind.

Because of death, I also wonder if that's why ghosts are a thing. There are definite boundaries between the living and the dead, yet I also want people to understand the forces of the not-yet-born. Linguistically, there is a cryptic message and meaning in that term, the not-yet-born.

When we read hyphenated words, it can mean they are primarily linked ideas that are connected, yet separate. We know that the word 'not' implies that something isn't another. The word yet is the number 'one' in the Cantonese language, and born has a context of birthing children. Even if not in the concept of conception or birth, there is a premise.

A born-again Christian may be the next incarnation of a living person. Those who have not been reborn mix the term not-yet-born as a wish and curse for me. Some people may wish I be born again, yet at the same time I'm alive on Earth, and I wish not to die to go to Heaven. I also urge that I can't fully grasp my admittance to Heaven or presume I'll be a father.

If there is a unified Heaven, then that realm is divine and explicitly the best things, people, and situations for all people. I'd think that Heaven has a collective heart, desires, and soul, and my understanding of Heaven is a place where all people have their most fantastic wants, and experiences manifest. It's a place where each other bolsters, strengthens, and magnifies those wants and experiences further. My version is an exponential and potentially infinite expansion of synergistic and divine unity, peacefulness, and bliss.

Heaven can be considered the ultimate best for *every* person, though on Earth, we're working together to allow each person their own divine experience. Singularly, as people, we have our likes and dislikes, though we remember the fact we're not the only people in existence. We can create our utopias, and guild with others who are building theirs, though it's the religious concept of Heaven that shuts off all other living things that might not fit into that mould.

Is that where Christianity would say that once we cut off all attachment to Earth, we go to Heaven? If that's true, I'm not entirely sure I'd like to do that because I still wish for a life on Earth to not be cut short. There are some fantastic people on Earth, and I wonder what would be different if we weren't here.

I've been pushing for meaning by attempting to be vital for those on Earth, yet is it that my soul is urging for purpose so that I don't pass off into the afterlife? Are fear and concern about death and the afterlife what motivates me to keep pressing the keys to assure a continued life on Earth? We're told 'God's will be done,' and I'm not God; I'm a human holding my micro and macrocosmic wishes.

When it was 2:16 AM and I had a flash of happiness and truth confirmed by the sound of a message on my phone (Christy's email), I took it as a signal that life is on track, *and* I've been doing the correct things. Then when I start writing and dive into my presumed ideas, I feel uncertain that my work has any meaning at all.

If my work is meant to impact the world, would I not be more successful and be aware of a positive effect from it? Or, is this part of the incubation process? It may be I'm to birth works and books to help those on Earth and the pieces of the puzzle that haven't lived yet.

I heard that time exists so that everything doesn't happen at once. We also have been told things need time to occur, yet the Law of Attraction and some spiritual guides have promised miracles can happen instantaneously. Some show us too that time can be shifted, twisted and turned in our favour. Is that God giving the blessings, or is it the Universe? Where is the balance of control and allowing?

If science is right, then what is left to assist us towards the fact that every letter, word, message, and even video is a pact some have made to those living? What about the links to Heaven and the afterlife and the direct connections from those angels like how Christy affects us? If Christy is a link to my divine network of people on Earth, and she and I are both linked to Heaven, then is it not the Global Organized Distractions that tell us when our paths have crossed?

The ways amaze the rays of a son that reminds his Dad that a Mother needs to stay on Earth to let her orbit with him around the sun. Each person values different things, yet if Universal concepts are valid and accurate for *all* people, then would that not apply to entities and attributes of the past, present, and future?

Some people have died and are guiding us and our future generations from a place physically separate. They may cognitively link our consciousness, yet these beings also may assure we need not pass off the mortal soil of Earth. If people are in Heaven, they might also wish and hope we can have such wondrous lives as they have while staying on Earth.

While those who've passed may feel sad for leaving others behind, perhaps some in Heaven wish we were with them to love again and try to pull us through the ether to their afterlife. The living also can be enjoyed so strongly on Earth that others don't take us away from the living world.

Death may call for some to pass off and on, yet that can also be a motivation to live even more vigorously. We know some are afraid of dying, and yet others may desire to take their own life. People that have tried to commit suicide have failed with substantial reasons assuring they stay on Earth.

For me, when I slashed my wrist, I thought of my parents and how I don't want to leave them behind. For some others, they too might need to be reminded that there are some shards and shreds of purpose and meaning they may need to share with Earth. Heaven can exist here, in the living realms for us, and I believe Christy helps the process so that we find perfect and divine moments in living life; she has done that for me.

Our awareness of the divine, while being a living conduit for it, instills hope, faith, and truth, and it's the reminder that we all are unlimited beings that can bring Heaven to our lives. From the Lord's Prayer, I've gleaned meaning that the Kingdom of Heaven is meant to exist on Earth too, and though I can't comprehend the separate realms of the literal Heaven and Hell, it's my wish and prayer that others also may exist on Earth in a heavenly state.

I've seen the birds flying through the sky as I exist in Heaven, and I have seen people walk up from the underworld as if from Hell. I am yet alive now. The wish, hope, and prayer are that I'll be active in the year 2053; alive and saying Earth may be considered the middle ground.

Purgatory can separate everyone's deepest fears and most fantastic fantasies. The tipping point is when we realize that our intrinsic wants and truths reveal whether we pass from overdosing on life or enduring through time. I would prefer to persist over time. Others too may find their insights into how to live like they are in Heaven while still alive on Earth.

Thank you, Christy! You've helped me find a purpose statement! I was online and heard my phone 'bling,' and it was your email. I read the email and then thought to write my thanks and response to the question "do you think creating Heaven on Earth is possible?"

Christy has been an exceptional online mentor for me for a few years now, and this chapter is a slightly modified version of the email I wrote that night. My previous depth of purpose was "to provide." The clarified message is that I want to provide Heaven to those alive while they are on Earth.

Helping people with food, water, and shelter is an

objective, yet I also want to give hopes, goals, and dreams. I may not yet know the point in time where I pass off from the realms of the living, yet if I am isolated and alone at the computer, can I still share? Yes.

Is writing books and emails the pathway to allowing people to like and love their lives? I don't know. Will others even read this? I don't know. Also, if people don't, Christy's message still planted the seeds for this chapter.

After the video:

After hearing what Christy and Martin Rutte shared, I recalled Christy is Italian. *Molto grazie* means thank you very much, or more specifically many graces. The wish is you pray.

If we agree that Heaven is a state of being and that we all can have access and grant other people's Heaven on Earth, then I'm reminded to breathe. Rewind to the question, "Do you think creating Heaven on Earth is possible?" I don't think we can *create* it, though we can positively assure we *allow* it to thrive.

We also can choose and create things that will infuse elements of what allows others and ourselves more heavenly moments. I liked how Martin talks about how the Torah didn't have a translation of a one-way departure from the Garden of Eden. It reminded me, as they both said, how people can choose to be or live in heavenly ways or states of being.

The word 'amazing' also trips in here how we can know the entire pathway of the maze and go back into the labyrinth to help bring people through to Heaven again. The idea of life being a maze alludes to an intuition. Forces that have found divine bliss or freedom can help others lost towards their places of joy and happiness.

Some rooms in the maze may be filled with sadness or chaos, though if we can bring each person into alignment and allyment, we may find a common ground of peace, love, unity, and respect.

With feelings and emotions, there is a saying: "That that carves deep into the heart with sadness can only be again filled with joy." What then of those that have been through Hell on Earth that can help guide and direct people back to Heaven on Earth?

In my 'before' comments, I didn't recall to mention the credo or prerogative of PLU8R. Although maybe not a total solution of Heaven on Earth, if we can activate global PLUR we'll be moving a lot closer to a cohesive experience. Global PLUR is Peace in every nation, Love for every race, Unity of every creed, and Respect for every religion.

The concept can be a compass of sorts, yet also is intrinsic as a value system. From the before part too, if a religious or spiritual realm of Heaven is separate from the existing domain we're in, then those who have passed onto Heaven may be those guides nudging or drawing us through the maze of Earth towards them.

Some people (yes, like me) want to stay trapped in the labyrinth and also want to help people find their rooms of divine happiness. I may have teetered on the edges of being sent to the afterlife, yet as I sit here at home isolated and highly aware, I don't want to think about the concept of a religious or spiritual war.

I remind us of an idea about the word *aware* and its potential hyphenation; *a-war-e*. When we are an 'extra' of war, we may not be on the main stage or in battle, yet our consciousness is still pervading. Or, if the religious texts are right and the war is already won, then how can we heal the world and reverse the damage done to the lives, societies, and wellbeing of Mother Earth? Can we remedy and assure another war need not occur?

There are battles and conflict in the world, and if each person upheld, expanded, and strengthened bonds of PLUR and PLU8R as a responsibility (the second R of PLU8R), maybe the concept of a full representation of Heaven on Earth will more justly manifest.

If our world of Earth is just one tiny planet in an entire

cosmos of time, space, and matter (recalling in the E=MC² equation the speed of light (instant miracles)) then maybe another soul might not need to wait 16 billion years only to reach Heaven on Earth.

What if there are alien or extraterrestrial beings that have an alternate concept of what Heaven is? Is Heaven a human concept, or is there a universal version of Heaven? If we are alive, we are conscious, and we may choose how we act, react, or respond.

If we are aware and not an extra of war, does that mean we must battle for the Kingdom of Heaven on Earth? What if Heaven is a Kingdom and Earth is one of its subjects locked in orbit around a star that was colonized by a single thought?

What if we on Earth are just a dream in the minds of another being and are purely immaterial and just kicked like a pebble into the cosmic dance of life? What if they discovered our planet and are using us as a petri dish to see how our cultures intermingle like sands through the hourglass? Or, if we take a solipistic perspective, how can we assure that we live another day if we feel we're ready for Heaven?

I hope I am ready for Heaven, just that I need not fall into the hands of Death to reach it. It is a bold choice for some to choose life and the betterment of the world of Earth. Not in comparison to other planets or even other people, yet instead our journeys of self-discovery and empowerment to guide, nurture, and tend the seeds of hope, love, and prosperity.

We increase the chances of others to remain on Earth and find their versions of Heaven while alive too. Thank you, Christy, for the link. I appreciate you, your friends, family, network, and followers for helping me with this. It may be an unclear antecedent and a sly joke that few get, yet thank you for reminding us that we can have it all, that we always have had it all.

Though, if we're not right enough with ourselves, and the world, to allow ourselves Heaven on Earth, we must reconnect it with life. Ti amo! Io sono un pazo per voi!

I MUST TELL YOU TOO

I realize that this book wasn't in the printed form yet, and set in some ways I may have been. I'm learning how to walk my talk and share God's words and works. I'm also quite Earthy so am not seeking to land in Heaven.

Like I typed in Christy's chapter, I believe we also can find Heaven on Earth and draw some people out of their Earth-Hells. I've understood and accepted I'm a vassal, and as I have climbed from the pit before; there are crisp reminders that cling to my mind.

We don't earn Salvation, yet in gratitude, we are granted it. I am compelled to share works and words in ways that shall call others to navigate through our Heavenly maze. The days in the two weeks before this had me in bed early. I again, though, explore the night with depths of my devotion. I recommend a vital book by Jack Canfield called *The Success Principles*.

I had edited the first chapter of *Fragments of Intent* the night I bought Jack's book for a friend. Earlier in the day I had manually revised the second chapter of *Etched in Stone*, and have been split between different works like an A.D.D. thing. I appreciate being able to break between projects when I reach a wall, though.

When I wrote this part, Nat's beauty was radiating

through my smile. Smiles from her keep the tears wept kept in a flask to remind me I also need to get Lewis' book *The Mask of Masculinity*.

I have neglected to pursue some of the urges of my heart. My recordings are still part of the process, and an odd twisted idea in my thoughts is that my music shall expand. I think the way I've said I'm 'cart before the horse' implies how my books are where I'm the workhorse, and my tracks are what I should be carrying.

Perhaps God does and has siphoned and ciphered my tracks while the books hold His ideas to assure the foundations may place. "Cycling parameters spin to a sphere because a linear direction is all that you hear." Time is a one-way linear form. The premise is the recordings are made and then *set* in stone as pieces of time and rhyme that God built me to form. Do we still construct and find future homes for others and ourselves?

The recording on the stereo at this point was *Stolen Thought*. It alluded that Natalie's the boss and I'm the vassal performing work for *her* world, even if she and I are not to couple. There are so many weird and wonderful twists that seem to purge me into belief while surging me forward with a release and relief it's not a choice I must make.

The pathway leads up to the door of the home. The garden on the left holds the pond outside the master bedroom, and the glass walls on either side of the house allow those inside to see out. Perhaps the two-way directivity of glass needs to be protected.

The vaulted ceilings above the pit hold two ceiling fans that keep the air moving in the house, while the wall case of books in the main office stem from the first vision I saw of the home. The shelves hold five hundred books that I've read while the desktop is extensive with a corkboard on the wall behind. Photos of my family and our travels are pinned up to remind me of our fun and love.

We host visitors twenty to thirty times a year, though these visitors gather to work on their relationships, businesses, and creative projects. With the support of my wife and myself, two to three-day visits with those we've met gather. We've met these people on our travels, and some are friends that find their way from different parts of Earth.

The home is safe and secure and located in Australia. Providing Point was my commitment in 2018, though I hadn't gathered the community together with my intents to provide. There is some money going to Chilliwack still from the book sales, yet I could not 'solve' the situation as I had intended on my own.

In July 2018, I accepted my meanders around points of place and time that are not cemented firm and fettered to faith. Instead, my heart needed to be tethered to fate and be free to be snacked around the spools of CDs that hold my being. I saw that I had been pushing for the purpose by wanting to provide instead of sharing love more truly with people that reciprocate care.

I found my way to earning another car, Colin helped me get the floor plans ready, and in 2024, the home's construction began. I remembered to heed my instincts and intuitions, and like how Taylor reminded me to focus thought upon what I want. I reminded myself to not push *for* the purpose, yet rather to *have* meaning and use.

The Fountains seemed not to be providing the waters of life, yet perhaps it was because the glaciers needed to melt to give their vital energy. I committed to the process again, and with the thread of this work coursing into my purpose driven promises, we met the completion of *The Fountains of Fortitude*.

Fortitude is a tricky thing and subject; the consequences of decades are substantial, yet only fragments of eternity. I wish to wield and yield millennia of time into the space of one rhyme, yet the ladder may have been up against the wrong wall.

I couldn't return my gratitude of being given what I've received immediately. It took a few years since the first Fountain called my whims and wants into the dominoes of our consecration. Each grain of sand from yesterday fueling how the sand had yet to be silt, and then shaped to clay.

Home is a place to connect a loved idea. A car wasn't fair for me to have at the point of no regular job and no books sales, yet as my audience expands it results in a just situation. Regarding time and activity, the Catacombs, Heath, and Flats are good nodal points, yet where else other than Decades and Waves can we have coffee in Chilliwack?

From a different fragment of time *2204 miles to go before landing and picking up a carton at Duty-Free. 40k feet in the air right now. Who's there?*

Resurface some previous codal activities too. I develop the card types for people such as how artifacts are kind, fresh, and vital, and there are reminders to value them more for who they are as people. With contialitic function starting, we contact love and heart and can call the Khan or Shard truth. Though it may not make sense, be absolute with *have to do* orders and operations. 4:15 is the destination. I took my meds, psychosis sucks, and we keep our health and strengthen the plucks.

This work drifted into the moments of rhyme. I chose to adjust my path to refuse music in a different way and definition. During the 2018 Festivus trip, my recordings seemed to seep out of my consciousness into the mental and visual fabric. Tapestries of the skies hold the glowing orbs, yet they also keep my soul.

I was a chemical addict pressing the keys and boundaries of ability and permission, yet I may have returned to burning through the night. It was July 16th, 2018. Kyle and I agreed that I'd adopt Zeus.

There may be only one more chapter remaining in *Open to Fate*, yet creations stem. I give my heart, and I ask for a return. Please let us gather around the fire again in 2019 and find the threads wound from the sound.

A digital stitch puts my thoughts back on the Internet. It may be I sandwich my work. Much music as the bread, the books as the middle, though I'm not clear how *my* music is a layer of nourishment. I tend to think human interaction is part of the bread.

Regarding the Sprites, let them fly free. The Sprites may need us to find our ways to navigate through the shared maze, yet this is meant to twist into how the shards hold fragments of their own. Starbucks? Honour and respect the baristas and shops fully. Keep from overloading people with work and be active in connection to form a PLU8R inversion into the conversion of text.

The revision and restructuring are solid ideas concerned about the used and reused edits of the first Fountains. If some say that promises from God more than a decade ago *are* part of His plan, then I shall relish and relevate in the luxury of allowing fate to occur. Messages from decades ago assist the web of time wrapping around sound.

The dreams from when we were children are still unfolding into the magnification of our deepest wants of love. I'm not God, so I don't know so much about all the secrets of the Universe. I do, though, remind myself that God directs us by using my writing and recording to tell me what the truth is.

There is a drastic difference in who I am since when I started this sentence from when I heard the first look. The tasted intuition found tuition of the fission and fusion from *Hold the Bond*. What is the next chapter I edit?

The contraceptive moments of rhyme have been preventing some seeds from slipping into the felt tip. Chip the mp3 to cue me up to sup, and tell me secrets of love's circles and punctuation of the pup. Scattered games find alphabetic notions of wisdom and direct guidance, and it does seemed more natural to plow the fields of text at night alone. What of the harvests when people gather as a collective and then sell the wares at the market?

For those that help sell the books, thank you, though how shall you be compensated? As my books gather earnings as seeds that we may share in the gardens, this strews through the starship from a familial drip. Would a kind tip be what she wishes for to open the core?

A pause of time may not reverse, yet as we disperse *The Sands of Yesterday* out into the world, a curled up kitten shares the written for how I've bitten the line. I take in a sign that makes the line trine up three points to one. The vinyl spun, yet I'm not The Son who you accused me to be.

I'm me, one who's set to see the ocean meet the glee and joy of the eyes of my baby boy, yet toy the web of the modes of text. If you think of a small case 't,' then see how that letter is a cross. Even those who are an atheist, agnostic, or have a non-Christian religion, most of them know that the cross signifies Christ. With the words 'the Truth,' see how the word *the* can separate to *t-he*. The cross and the male pronoun 'he' without space. It's a definite article to note.

If we add spaces to different words, shards of language start to confuse and clarify. I'd like to assure the cross is a part of the world, yet if I start at the top and drop down to the bottom, think of adding 'L' for love into The Word, and you have The World.

"From the left, right, front, back, hack into the mainframe. Program selected name."

The Glass House has kept me up at night. I couldn't sleep one night because I was envisioning the home, so I went to the computer to write more in this book. Returning, though, I found the cryptic and caustic beverage in the same cup from which I drink.

I'm inclined to write more at night, yet the chemicals contaminate. There is a drastic pull between thinking healthy choices are not what my heart desires and a belief my substances are crucial to my creative development. Am I condensing time's crystals and compressing my future timelines with drugs?

I completed the Fettered Faith version of *Etched in Stone*. The Healing Hearts version of *Fragments of Intent* wasn't done yet, though. My recordings are part of this, though I'm approaching two decades of recorded work without many sales either. My books are only two to three years old, yet they may still expand. Both crafts hold an evolution of ability, though what shall be the third strand to braid them together?

Julianna talked to me and told me that although we may not know the next steps, it's best to keep open to ideas and opportunity. Though we don't know what the future holds, we also must have faith we'll find our next steps. For Julianna, she knows what's most important to her, her kids. I don't have kids at this point, yet know my work is what I must nurture and nourish. My concern is that the chemicals are parenting this work.

I've not had a job in the past two years, though I have planted some seeds in the community and cosmos. My faith is chained to the present moment as I tend to blame God for what happens when I don't understand. Some psychologists would accuse us of creating our unknown selves, and there are parts of myself that expose and embarrass me without a conscious reaction or comprehension.

I have an idea that a lot of what I know as absolutes may not yet be perceived. My fears have tried to gnaw into my psyche, and subtle allusions of death creep into consciousness eluding my forgotten stone. The stability of my faith waivers from nil to repentant energy and attitude with defiant wishes to thrive.

I best not defy God. He knows me better than I could ever tell another. Fragments of my mind siphon a lost potion of denial, yet I shift to urge the smiles not to struggle. There is despair woven in the thread, yet we almost recall the walls that hold many in, and almost everyone out.

As of August 2018, the sprouts of *Seeds of Tomorrow* were few. I thought I was going to provide great things for a vast number of people, though at that same time, I seemed not even to have produced an assurance I shall live.

I don't want to be defiant or dismissive, yet I yearn and wish to thrive. I have refused to submit to the displayed results I'd yet formed, yet we've not gathered even ten patrons to Providing Point. I thought my books would be an income source to house people, yet less than twenty books have sold on Amazon as of September 2018.

I wonder if you see these shifts in my writing; from fantastic faith to the fears of a fatalistic wraith. I twist between believing all things are possible to think there is no other possible way. Deterministic belief in fate, to again wondering if it's even worth it for me to create.

I've met a point in my bookwork where I trust the process of typing and revising and refining. I wonder if I must and need to grind if any goodness shall come from what I've written. Is it delusion or sheer determination that allows destiny to hold the plow?

I wonder if it's because I refuse to understand that I still need to tell you. I'm not a saviour or Christ, and I'm paranoid people want to end my life for not believing in proclaiming religious or spiritual ideas. I wonder if death has been hounding me and pushing messages into my awareness that Earth doesn't want me here.

If Earth doesn't want me here, I also add I'm not a righteous or holy person that wants to go to Heaven. I don't wish to go to Hell either, though maybe it's then again how I'm a coward for not wanting to go to war. I'm accurately far too passive to push for any cause, even, it seems, the protection of my own life.

Is that how this book is *Open to Fate*? I open a moment of time also to open my lack of understanding and comprehension. I reveal a willingness to surge dreams to do something to change the course of events on Earth, and I'm only one person. Since I'm not God or have magical powers, I also remind myself of the will of all that is drastically beyond the influence of my waning heart.

I seem not to have praised God, though am meekly thankful that I'm allowed to live and be. Perhaps there is repentance to be made for how this world develops. I seem to think reparations must prepare many sources of life. That might be part of the next Fountain's journey.

WHAT'S YOUR BIG IDEA?

Even if people can't always actualize their own 'big idea,' I think each should have one. If you do have a big idea, put it on paper or into a file and share it with someone! That's what this chapter is for me.

Introversial and Providing Point are two of my seeds, though I've not tended or activated them correctly. I'd like to share how the ideas expand and share the vision of how they can affect Earth. People make things. Some of those people also are givers and wish to help. Providing Point is my big idea, though Introversial is my tiny branch of it.

Introversial is using Patreon, a crowdfunding site, to gather pledges for providing locally on street level. The premise and promise of Providing Point are to provide food, shelter, and water for people. The big concept is to provide for *all* people and should not be limited just to Chilliwack. It's a transferrable idea for other creators.

My work includes premises I've gleaned from online mentors. I committed to giving part of my book and music earnings from a Gary Vaynerchuk principle of giving; 51%/49%. Lewis Howes was the first person that showed me the idea of providing something to a massive number of people; in his case to inspire people 100 million people to earn a full-time income doing what they love. I learned from

Water.org that near one billion people don't yet have access to clean and safe water, and Christy Whitman seeded the idea that we are unlimited and can achieve anything. Jack Canfield teaches the principles of how to succeed, though I mixed all these ideas up, and on August 2nd, 2018 made another shift and pivot.

Providing Point's Introversial branch is creatively just my books and music at that point. All earned beyond Patreon and PayPal fees gathered through Introversial's Patreon page goes to others for Share and Care cards as of July 2018. I give digital books and music as rewards for pledging, though I've not pushed strongly enough for pledges up to now. I don't like mooching money, so had believed I could entice people to contribute because of access to the books.

There is a multi-win if all the Patreon earnings go to others. If people want to contribute to the cause, their generosity provides efficiently. They receive books and music as a reward, and as we share books, the ideas of Providing Point expand through readership.

Ideas proliferate. As part of the books' sales earnings go to charitable work, the more that purchase books, the more we may provide to the causes. The more earned via Providing Point also allows additional viewership, and if people choose to read or play the reward items, we can help involute the work outwards.

If others made their work and commitment to providing for people in their local communities, there could be other Providing Points in other cities and towns. If other creators pledge part of their earnings or provide their work and art to Providing Point patrons, we can provide more.

Providing Points in other communities can provide for different causes, and gatherers can work with other artists, authors, and musicians to share their material with patrons. Though Providing Point is the overarching program and name, it's not yet so much of a legally bound non-profit. We've not gathered enough to register governmentally.

Up to October 2018, Providing Point is 4x Patrons and

me. I'm working to find a Shared Freedom Solution as the concept is to ensure we take care of all people. One person at a time, Introversial's branch began in Chilliwack. We may create, gather audience and pledges, and share earnings, though what I need to remember more often is I also need to provide love and care.

Would other people want to glean from creators sharing their work via Providing Points? It may be a mutual benefit. If we can gather more works and share them for pledges, creators can expand their audience. We may assemble and collect more creators and contributors, and we can share and provide a more diverse catalogue of creative works for patrons.

If we can encourage more pledges, we can expand the number of reach via patrons, and an increase in the potential audience for artistic contributions can lead to additional exposure and support for creators. We can increase the number of people who know about the artists, the artists may sell more of their work, and the causes they work for shall glean more awareness and earnings via patronship.

When in my creative process and understanding, I shift my commitments, and I restate some premises and promises. As of August 3rd, 2018, I committed to sharing 100% of the individual Fountains earnings to different causes and charities. If a portion of my work's profits goes to various purposes, I think we can do more in the form of giving.

I'd like to help the homeless and low-income people in town, though I'd also like to share with other people who need or want support too. Part of my cause is improving Earth and not just the Fraser Valley. Similar to the chapter *Buckle Up Koyich* in the 6th Fountain, I must share my promises.

I have gotten edgy, insecure, and nervous when I reach these points of commitment, yet keep at it. I know I'm doing good work, and I remind myself of concepts I believe. I push past with faith that we have gotten this far into the process of the Fountains books.

My obsessive compulsion carries a lot of this. I know if we earn sales and gain patrons I'd feel more fulfilled too. I sometimes have felt stagnant and believed I'm wasting my time, effort, and energy, though I keep writing even if it's not rational.

I must repent for not activating Providing Point in Chilliwack to success yet as of October 2018. I've not wanted to mooch money or pledges and I'd not marketed my books and music well up to that point. I've lacked drive, ambition, and the motivation required, and I also must atone for not being active on street level getting to know more people.

I need to reach out more frequently to people, and I've been a star-crossed waffle who's dealing with some of my mental health issues and recovery. Since this is the closing chapter of this Fountain and you may not have read previous ones, I want to condense and summarize the Fountains up to now.

The Fountains started with me wanting to meet Natalie Imbruglia. I started the first book *Finding Natalie* wishing to share the book with the world so that she would come and meet me. I intended on writing the entire book from her perspective, yet fell from that after the first chapter. I picked up voices of a few other people in the second chapter and then wrote outwards to Natalie and the world of Earth.

The second book, *Searching for Tomorrow* was me starting to think about what I was going to do if I didn't meet Natalie. I started plotting and planning and using gimmicky marketing tactics with the intent to earn money through writing. I included a chapter written to Gary Vaynerchuk at the close of the book, as he was my primary guidepost at that time with online learning. It also was part of my process in developing proficient authorship.

From the Valley to the Fountain started with the remembrance of my first believed love, the Original Lovestone; Althea. I shared thoughts about my chemical habits and also a bit about my tainted past. I wrote the book trying to push my purpose and dreams, and also the Natalie dream away. Perhaps I am stubborn as a mule and free as a lark as one chapter said.

I combined the first three Fountains book into a compilation titled *Fragments of Intent*. It was the first substantial book that I released as the first three individual Fountains were training grounds for learning how to write and publish. The book went through some drastic revision and the final version rereleased in October 2018. Two thirds of the 3rd Fountain didn't reach the completed version.

It was the three-part book *The Sands of Yesterday* where we started to grip in. Although I had the idea of the Seed Fund when writing the 3rd Fountain, the 4th, 5th, and 6th Fountains honed my craft and started to germinate my faith. I released a few different versions of the books as I learned how to edit, revise, and improve my books. Although the Unlimited texts formed individually, they have gathered into their current available and final forms. The post-Unlimited copies gathered into *The Sands of Yesterday*, and the last revision resulted in the Sanctified Spirit version of that book.

The 7th Fountain, *Etched in Stone*, is the Fountain before this one. It also is in a post-Unlimited form and starts the three-part compilation *Shards of my Soul*. The version that you see now is how I've allowed myself to become. I put a wish out of the Universe to guide me and let me heed the forces of Heaven and Hell. I open my control to the hands of Fate.

Other authors also don't always know whom they channel, and that's part of my mystery too. I think I wrote this, yet I know I haven't. By the point this text reaches you, it's gone through revisions that changed it from its initial sequence and series.

But what is my big idea? I've thought to earn and share abundance for others and myself when it seems I'm in total lack. How can I make enough money to afford a basic living wage for myself, let alone a thousand other people? How can I wish and decree that Providing Point could house the entire population of homeless in the Fraser Valley when we only have $18 a month pledged?

I believe that forces of fate and destiny are using me as a conduit for global significance even if I'm isolated and alone most of the time. I understand that higher powers have massive reach and have thought they are secretly conspiring to allow me to thrive instead of smiting me for being a dramatically flawed human.

I believed Earth was going to be destroyed Christmas 2017. I also thought that the one I fell for in 1998 had wished me to be dead to meet her in Heaven. If Zeus is angry that Jesus took over the role of a primary person to be worshiped, then how have I been so daft not even to speak that I too believe in God and pray to Him?

I have been allowed to exist here in moments radical thankfulness to be alive. I also believe I'm not the standard human suited to live in society. If I can find happiness and feelings of intense love for others when I'm isolated and alone, why haven't I shown appreciation and voiced it to ask a real girl for a dance? If Natalie wasn't my soulmate, then why am I still thinking of her twenty years later while believing she wishes I knew the truth?

I still don't know.

I don't want to close this book with declarations and wishes for the future. I also don't want to make claims of false truth or audacious accusations. I want to know how these books are valuable to people even if they aren't a commercial success. I'd love and adore to know if Providing Point is an idea to pursue or if I should release it as unsuccessful. I still desire to know what my purpose is and what I can do to share and feel love.

I have been working towards a living legacy, yet I feel like I have so few to speak with and that people are avoiding me. The cat is fantastic, and I like that he's here, so perhaps that's part of this. My spiritual comprehension and parental influence also remind me that I have work to do. If I want to have a life of prosperity and abundance, it won't always magically happen. There are miracles; Zeus is right of that. I also now know I learn to live *with* someone, not merely *for* them.

A selfless attitude and ethics are a neat thing, though many others have also told me that they think I should work entirely for just my benefit and earnings. Gratefulness and reciprocation allure me into moments of play. When working on my projects, I've found disturbingly good moments of clarity, and my obsessions remind me what is right, at least for me.

I don't know what's best for others, let alone myself. I shall continue to thrive, create, and give, though I also must not do good things just so that good things happen to me.

"The right thing, at the right time, for the right reason."-Owen Beattie

I must also remember to do so for the *right people.*

ACKNOWLEDGMENTS

The world of Earth uses us as conduits and channels of understanding. I'm meekly and boldly thankful to know I am not alone. Even if solitary with this work, I sense spirits and energies that remind me of my wishes from more than a decade ago. It's how our hearts entwine.

I thank all forces of life for allowing me the grace to create, and though at a near glacial pace, I'm also thankful to trace the lines of spines left along the shores of space. The premise of being aware (a-war-e) also has me grateful I need not be a soldier in a physical battle.

My battles of consciousness, morality, and addiction forge these books in different ways, and through the maze, they reverse the curse. A nurse's call walled to my being, yet I'm also dearly thankful we see some of the fields bloom.

The luxuries I've received are predominantly not understood by myself, yet creative freedom, artistic patience, and cosmic guidance are valued. I pray well that others may have such magnificent blessings for themselves too.

The best that I may do at this point is to keep forging the text and revising my soul so that the shards may blend. We're content to amend with every friend, lover, and entity in a world of which to tend.

Thank you for reading, and explicit thanks to my parents, cousins, uncles, aunts and otherwise plus the Khans, Shards, Contialitic Guides, and the Communities and Consects. You each allow me to do what I do.

Peace, Love, Unity, and infinite Respect
Robert Koyich.

ADDITIONAL INFORMATION

Fragments of Intent - From the First Three Fountains
The Sands of Yesterday (The Second Three Fountains)
Shards of My Soul (The Fountains of Fortitude)
Mosaic of Miracles (The Fountains of Fantasy)
The Waters of Life (The Fountains of Flourishing)
Winds of Change (The Fountains of Divinity)
The Sacred Spirit (The Fountains of Attuned Hope)
A Tree of Life (The Fountains of Reflection)

My Bag of Trips (My History, Story, and Experiences with
Drugs and Psychosis)

Shared Node (Key to Me)

Please go to **www.ProvidingPoint.com** to assist with providing
groceries via reloadable grocery cards.
OR
Scan this QR code to donate via Donorbox

All donations will receive a valid tax receipt

To email Rob, please message Robert@RobertKoyich.com

Learn, Love, Live, Thrive, Create, Play, and Pray
PLU8R

Manufactured by Amazon.ca
Bolton, ON

45116854R00058